To Gemma

Love Mum

27th Feb. 2016.

In the Long Run

Rob Burn

In the Long Run

The humorous story of
a marathon runner

Pelham Books

First published in Great Britain by
PELHAM BOOKS LTD
44 Bedford Square
London WC1B 3DU
1983

British Library Cataloguing in Publication Data

Burn, Rob
In the long run.
I. Title
PR6052.U/

ISBN 0 7207 1446 X

Photoset by Alacrity Phototypesetters, Banwell Castle, Avon
Printed in Great Britain by Hollen Street Press Limited, Slough
and bound by Hunter & Foulis, Edinburgh

For Pat, Lucy, Becky and Tom

Contents

Part Two

Part Three

I have always firmly attributed my desire to run a marathon to my inability ever to finish things.

As long as I can remember, beginning the most horrendous ventures has never held dread for me. Even activities of which I have little knowledge — and there are many — I have tackled with gusto, only eventually to run out of enthusiasm before the task has been completed. I have, for example, the world's greatest collection of first chapters of books, plus a multitude of inventions which would change the course of history if I could only get them off the drawing board. Even my house, after surviving for over two hundred years, has suffered terribly during the last ten from unfinished attacks to its structure.

Then it struck me like a bolt from above that to run a marathon was a panacea for this character defect. After all, there is only one way to find out if you can run a marathon, and that is to go out and run one. If you can you can, and if you can't — well, you leave it at that or you have another go another time. But 3 or 4 hours after beginning the race you have categorically, undeniably finished and there can be no half measures about it.

So I did the first London Marathon on 29 March 1981. It was Mother's Day and the clocks went forward one hour, just to make things a little bit more difficult. I had only given myself three months to get fit enough, which was an absurdly short period of time and ridiculously arrogant of me. I had been sponsored by hundreds of people in the village, all proceeds to go to the local primary school. Should I finish, the school stood to gain upwards of £500. And on the Friday before the race I was invited by the headmaster to address the children as they sat on the floor in assembly. I was wearing all the appropriate running gear and I had to explain how I felt and why I was attempting to do such a strange thing. After I had finished they gave me three cheers, wished me good luck and then stood and sang 'Fight the Good Fight', and I wondered what they would all think of me if I failed to get round.

But I did get round. It took me 4 hours 18 minutes and I left both my knee joints somewhere between Tower Bridge and the Isle of Dogs. What did surprise me, though, both during the training and the marathon, was the highly emotional and creative side of all that foot slogging. It was something which I hadn't expected. It therefore shocked me as much as everyone else when I calmly declared that during 1982 I would like to run in the New York Marathon, write a book and make a film, which, in some very personal way, would record the chaos and the satisfaction which comes from the preparation and the event itself. Neither of these two documentaries would attempt to tell others how to prepare for a marathon. They were to be highly subjective and, in places, totally irrational, with a very thin dividing line between what was taking place inside and outside my head.

There is, in fact, no evidence that my 'training schedule', to use the term in its loosest, most jocular sense, was appropriate. I rarely consulted the many magazines or books which explain exactly what, when and how you should subject your body to the many hours of road running and exercises. Rather I trained for the marathon as one learns to ride a bike — in total ignorance but with strong determination. You keep on going until you fall off and damage yourself and then you just get up and start all over again. I set myself modest objectives and if I was able to achieve them, the next time I pushed further. It was a simple, almost naïve ritual. And when things went wrong, which they frequently did, I would sulk, ignore them or, if the problem was of a physical nature, consult a friendly physiotherapist and pour out my troubles to him.

Now all three challenges have been met: I have run in New York; the film has been shown on BBC Television; and the book is in print. So perhaps my prognosis was correct after all.

10

Acknowledgements

To Joan Thresher, for typing the many revised manuscripts.

To Lesley Gowers, for her enthusiasm and advice.

To Ruth Baldwin and Jeff Peters, for their suggestions on the text.

To Reebok Limited, especially Mike Bowles and John Ovenden, for support during training and the very practical matter of the excellent running gear.

To the New York Road Runners Club, who organised a truly remarkable event.

Part One

High Street, Banwell

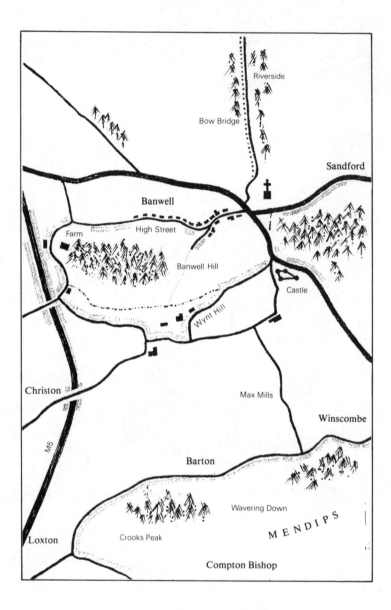

Chapter One

Reflections on my brief career as a top-flight athlete and my return to bad ways. The reality of the Brent Knoll Race. The decision is made to run in New York.

Saturday, May 30. I had accepted that my career as a top-flight athlete had been and gone since that memorable grey day in March 1981. In the two months following the London Marathon I had barely touched my running shoes, leaving them well alone under the bed gathering dust instead of speed. I thought that was the best place for them — out of sight, out of grind. I was happy with my medal, my article describing the race which had been published in a sports magazine the following month and my running number, 5254, which I had had framed and hanging on the wall for all to see within less time than it had taken me to run the race itself.

Since March, my body weight had shifted from a lithe 11½ stone, which for my height of 6 feet with my shoes on seemed to be as near perfect as it was ever likely to be, to a rather bulbous 12½ stone, and all in the space of the two months since the race — a growth rate of ½ stone per month. At this rate I should weigh around 15½ stone by Christmas!

I blame most of it on a planned relaxation programme of my own making, partly in England and partly in Holland. I may seem a little bold to claim the entire credit but it wasn't all tulips, roses and Edam. No, it took a concentrated effort to return to those old habits, the old pleasures. I was content with life in general: I had my studio to work in at home, and some interesting graphic work to do in it, designing this and that.

I had, however, come briefly out of retirement during a warm springlike morning in May. This was for an event called the Brent Knoll Race, a matter of some 5½ miles up, around and down a rather large lump of lias in the middle of the Somerset levels. The Knoll is a pleasant enough sight, even impressive as the sun sets behind it, 30 miles across the Bristol Channel, somewhere amongst the Welsh hills. This great bump on the landscape must surely have some religious or pagan history, like Glastonbury Tor, about 10 miles to the south-east. Yet romantic and beautiful as it is to look at and ponder over, it is no love sonnet to run up and that is the object of the Brent Knoll Race. Over streams, along deserted cow tracks — one is able to deduce that they are cow tracks — across a road or two and then on to the Knoll itself, supported by a handful of people who have probably seen it all before and who know what is about to happen to the 80-odd competitors who pass them.

Any lingering taste of glory that had remained within me after the London Marathon rapidly poured out that day, along with pints of sweat, as I began to ascend the hill which I swear would defeat many an aspiring mountaineer. The method was running, grunting and at one point even scrabbling on all fours, where the race rules regarding the illegal use of the hands to aid locomotion were totally ignored owing to an overwhelming desire to die. Up and up to the top I struggled, past the farms and bewildered animals, up the well-worn sheep track, my legs like uncooked frankfurters. And then from out of the air: 'Number, please.'

'What?' I groaned.

'Number, please. I can't see it,' said the same voice rather irritably, like an impatient telephone operator.

'Of course you can't see it,' I spluttered. 'I'm lying on it!'

I rose painfully, exposing my dripping number and then, as he wrote 'number 57' down on his check list of runners who had reached the top, he pointed and shouted, 'Thank you. That way round.'

And so I ran to the right, sidestepping the dead and the dying who littered the ¼-mile circuit on the summit of the Knoll. An inferior athlete on inferior oolite!

'Just think of the view,' cried one of the locals as I was passing; he was obviously from the Brent Knoll tourist board. 'The view!' I thought obediently. But my eyes were incapable of focusing, let alone picking out the natural beauties of the Somerset levels. I supposed that 20,000 years ago bone-waving, hairy, paleolithic man could have been found running up and down Brent Knoll without so much as a gasp in his quest for supper or to do nasty things to the hill dwellers. My mind wandered back and forth over several thousand years until I managed to regain a little dignity.

Then followed the descent, passing people on their way up, and that wicked primeval feeling, a mixture of 'rather you than me, mate' and laughter, as I hit the easy bit and they still had the agony to come. Many of them may still be there to this day as far as I know, but I finished a happy 33nd in 39 minutes. This had taken place some five weeks previously, however, and since then — nothing. Hardly a rush to the pub or a brisk Sunday morning walk with the dog along the rocky shore of Wood-spring Priory to break the idleness. So that was the status quo. And then Mark came round, Mark who works for a sports magazine in Exeter and for whom I had written the account of the London Marathon.

'What about running the New York Marathon and writing an article for us to print in the November issue?' he said. 'We'll cover the cost of the flight there, plus the hotel. Write what you want. Could be a laugh. What do you think?'

I reached for the bottle of Geneva which I had bought at the duty-free shop on the boat from the Hook twenty-four hours earlier, to be used with discretion during the coming months, and together, as the hours grew longer and the liquid in the bottle grew shorter, we laid plans for an autumnal romp around the Big Apple.

Chapter Two

Training recommences. The first few feeble excursions into the country-side. My first conclusive failure. My inability to make decisions is reviewed. A little regained self-respect and confidence. The medical relationship between running and catching influenza is considered. Training is resumed.

Sunday, May 31, 3 miles. I ceremoniously dressed, pulling on my sweat shirt and my rather worn running shorts, which appeared to have shrunk in my absence. I dusted off my running shoes which still bore the scars of the Knoll, or rather of the cow tracks which surround it, and went out into the morning air.

I was appalled at how quickly a body can degenerate into a wobbly, blubberous lump. My legs complained about such unsolicited haste and my lungs about the Dutch half-coronas which they had praised only a few days before. I ached all over, from my head to my toes. Unaccountably, even my bum began to ache like it had never done before and I could find no justification for that whatsoever. And the kids in the street began laughing and jeering at some old man trying to regain some of his past glory and how difficult it is to run with panache whilst clenching one's cheeks together.

I managed the 3 miles around Banwell Hill, reflecting on the ease with which I had achieved the same distance during my training runs earlier in the year. Today it had taken 30 minutes. I reached home with my head bursting and the blood pumping round my body as though I had too much of it and it was desperately seeking a way to get out. The sweat poured out of me as though I was leaking all over and I collapsed on the kitchen stairs, gasping for a lot of air and a little sympathy from my family who gazed at me over their breakfast cereals. I found it impossible to get either, although my 'faithful dog Dora' did lick my feverish forehead from time to time as the rest of the family went about their tasks, semi-oblivious to the pulsating blob that cluttered up the kitchen.

My next attempts made up a hat-trick of bad jokes. I could not imagine running one step further than the 3 miles which I had set myself on these trips. The incredible fact of running 26 miles kept returning as I struggled to keep one leg in front of the other, and the days which followed were accompanied by cramps, aches and a general pre-ageing syndrome.

Friday, June 5, 3 miles. Around Banwell Hill in the morning. It takes about 27 minutes, regardless of any contingencies such as weather, time of day or state of mind, but the effect is always the same: something between working in a steel mill and having your limbs torn off one by one by an overweight Sumo wrestler.

On the south side of Banwell Hill lies Wynt Hill which, when viewed from a motor car, is a pleasant enough incline. Some ¾ mile long, it falls about half way on the journey around Banwell Hill. Over the next few months it was to see the very worst side of me and no doubt came to regard me as a failure as a human being and an extremely rude and smelly one to boot. This, however, was mild in comparison to how I was to view Wynt Hill.

Knowing that I did have the ability to run longer distances worried me a little, and I was resolved to attempt a longer run soon.

Saturday, June 6, 4 miles. I thought it important to prove a point. Such rank bad form had to be stamped out at source, even if it made my legs ache to do it. I would show me who was boss. 'Robert,' I said, 'up and about what has to be done.'

So I ran out into the High Street to attempt a 6-miler. Around the hill, Max Mills, Winscombe and home past the castle. In my head all was clear to me. The afternoon was hot and clammy, one of those balmy days of early summer when an ordinary man can so foolishly give head space to false aspirations.

Within 2 miles I was a sack of damp smelliness. By the 4-mile mark my whole life seemed wet, hot and pointless and I stopped running, which was by far the most sensible thing that I had done that day and I could not for the life of me understand why I hadn't thought of it before. I walked for a short while. But as I slowly recovered a little breath, so I lost a little pride, until I felt a hopeless failure both physically and mentally.

I managed to regain a little hope for the future, however, by refusing a lift with a Somerset farmer who noticed my stilted motion from the solace of his tarted-up Cortina.

'Giv'n up, then?' he shouted, drawing level. 'Bain't yew ment ta run?'

'No, all part of training — run a bit, walk a bit, and so on,' I lied through my teeth.

'Oh, I thought yew wuz jus' tired,' he said astutely, drily or stupidly and drove off into the distance where I wanted to be. Such is pride, I thought, as I sank to yet another all-time low.

For a few days afterwards my humiliation and ailing conscience laid heavily upon me and, apart from the running, I stayed indoors and refused to talk to anybody.

Sunday, June 7, 7 miles. I set off down Riverside with that now oh-so-familiar feeling of not knowing where the hell I was going to end up. This is such a constant state of mind that I often wonder why I am not capable of making a decision before I leave the house. Why is it not possible for me to sit in the kitchen with a nice cup of tea and plan out my itinerary to the nearest mile or so, put on my running shoes and be off out? It is the same sort of indecision as I feel about making an appointment to see the bank manager or pulling in for petrol. It is something I just put off and off until I either get a 'Dear Mr Burn, I wonder if you would kindly call in to see me . . . ' or I end up walking half way home. It is obviously a fault in my make-up, not being able to face up to things, to predict the predictable or prevent the inevitable. I wonder if Pheidippides had this trouble? If so, he might have ended up in a town called Kalkis or Thivia rather than Athens and then that would have changed the course of history a little.

So I pointed me down Riverside. My legs resented being forced to go along with the rest of me, compelled by a decision which they felt had nothing to do with them, but still the body, the ultimate democracy, had its way and off we all went.

The Weston-to-Bristol road is 3 miles away. In the past, at the peak of my former fitness, such a distance had formed the starting point of a decent canter. Today I could swear on the Three As rule book that the Council had moved it further north since my last visit. I left the main road after a few yards and made for Way Wick, a fictitious-sounding place if ever there was one — and there is more than a grain of truth in that. The unsuspecting would certainly never find such a location should they have cause to search for it on a damp, misty autumn night.

Like many similar spots in Somerset, where the rhines and flat peaty fields meet beneath ageing willows, there is little variation in character to give the searcher a clue to his whereabouts. But the run is a pleasant one, away from the sounds of the main roads, past homesteads and small farms with such names as Redbrick Cottage and Stonebridge Farm, and over bridges across green algae-covered water with nothing to disturb the surface apart from the water boatmen and the ever-busy mosquitoes.

As I was passing some old orchards, an outing of the local ladies' horse society moved towards me. The riders passed me by, sharing the same haughty, suspicious glances as their mounts. There was absolute quiet apart from the noise of the eight or nine horses panting and their metal shoes on the dry road. Then suddenly the illusion of control and superiority was irretrievably shattered as the last chestnut gelding let forth a fart of such extraordinary depth and feeling that it made me falter and quicken my pace. The horse, by breaking wind and rank simultaneously, not only startled its rider, whose cheeks began rapidly to match the colour of the beast itself, but also a herd of young heifers who had been inquisitively moving along with the party on the other side of the blackthorn hedge.

I returned to Banwell down Wolvershill Road. What little energy I had reserved for the last 2 or 3 miles I had used up in my attempts to stop laughing and I felt weary and exhausted after the 7-odd miles. It had taken me about one hour but I had at last regained some self-respect, even if a certain lady from the local equine society had lost a little of hers.

Monday, June 8, 3 miles. Renewed confidence. This is the best way for me to describe what I felt as I began to run around Banwell Hill. The period of self-consciousness at being seen making what can best be described as 'a fool of oneself' seemed to have passed and I, to a point, began to ignore this aspect of training which turns many a budding athlete away from the track and into a profession less open to ridicule.

Yet if my spirit was strengthened, my legs certainly were not and after the 7 miles of the previous day, they ached and groaned as I plodded my way around in 27 minutes. I resolved to make an effort to strengthen them — after all, they were to do most of the work.

Tuesday, June 9, 8 miles. I telephoned a friend who sometimes takes it into his head to come with me on these saunters. Although I much prefer to run alone, the effort of deciding exactly where to go is so painful and time-consuming that sometimes unless I have the decision made for me, there is a strong possibility that I will never get out of the house at all. Where shall I suffer next? Over the hill perhaps? A bit of cross-country and that 1 in 3 rise up into the woods? God, that would be painful. What about Riverside and the cool air by the water? No, if I choose that I'm letting myself in for a 6- or 7-miler or more, and what happens if I run out of steam and can't get back again? Just round the village, then? Hardly worth the effort, might as well not bother. And so the relentless dialogue continues, getting me nowhere.

All day I have to make decisions; people expect me to do it with self-confidence and an unbiased eye. And then when I decide to do my own thing, take off on my own for an hour, what happens? I can't make up my mind, I sit in my kitchen and deliberate until I get asked to do some domestic task or make the children's tea or receive the 'Oh, back already? Can you see why the washing machine keeps flooding the bloody kitchen?' And then I have to rush outside and stand in the road looking like an ad for tracksuits until some whim or puff of wind lures me into positive action. But by this time I am so exhausted by all that mental agony and abuse from the kitchen, I feel as if I have run half a marathon before I start. So anguish of the mind is the first step in a long diary of discomfort.

This is why I was to be found calling on a friend. 'What about the Old Pier?'

He looked at me and said nothing for a while and I thought him to be ill.

'The Old Pier at Weston?' he said at last in horror. 'That's 10 miles away.'

'About 9,' I said.

'I thought we were going round the hill. I haven't run 9 miles for years — it'll kill me!'

'It won't.'

'It will.'

'We'll take it steady — just the job, get the podge down a bit, and anyway, I haven't been that far for ages so we can both suffer together.'

'Bloody liar. I saw you going off down Riverside the other day.'

'Not me.'

'It was, and you've been playing squash umpteen times a week.'

'I haven't for a while,' I say and so the banal banter, a runners' rhetoric, continues about the possibility of us both making the Old Pier without dragging our bums on the floor.

We set off. Richard is a fairly fit man of around thirty-seven. He has a high regard for personal endeavour and made the 120-mile journey to London to watch the marathon and give me moral support, although there was little morality in the choice of language he used for encouragement along those long, lonely miles between Tower Bridge and the Isle of Dogs. However, I was most grateful for his presence and that of his wife, Carol, as those few miles would have been more painful without it. He hopes to run himself next year, God, bones and the selection committee willing.

Riverside is a pleasant lane along which to run, with its shallow stream to the left, overhung with withy willow and at that time providing refuge for a fine pair of mute swans and eight tufty grey cygnets. As we passed they were sitting on the grassy bank, heads curled sideways and backwards. One of the adults had attacked my white VW 'Beetle' only a week previously, obviously under the impression that it was a larger intruding mute swan, and I therefore took a wide, cautious detour to the right, making what I thought to be friendly swan- or duck-type noises.

We followed the river, leaving the land and moving over the hard dried river path to Black Lock as a stoat shot out from one set of cover quickly to find another.

I was not fit. By any reckoning device I was not fit. It is not difficult to reach such a conclusion. Lack of fitness has its own way of letting you know. It sometimes lets you think that you are fit, just for a short while, say until you are about 3 or 4 miles away from the nearest telephone or resting place, and then it springs itself upon you suddenly, like the effects of a large scotch too early in the day. It usually makes for your legs first, removing all the muscles and bones quickly and efficiently; where it puts them I do not know, but remove them it does.

Within the space of a few hundred yards my legs had vanished, and I silently cursed my big mouth with its smart ideas of long, splendid evening runs. But I dared not stop: Richard would never have let me forget that one. I carried on, therefore, up through Worle, a curious village whose claim to fame is that it is one of the fastest-growing communities in Western Europe. Much of this instant town has the charm of a town planner's armpit, but the older parts are pleasant enough. We ran through the middle and up the winding lane that leads to the village of Kewstoke with its view of the Severn estuary and Sand Bay away to the right and the woods on the hill to the left, separating the quiet and the unspoilt from the extravagances of Weston.

After 6 miles we entered the woods on the toll road which leads from Kewstoke along the shallow cliffs to the Old Pier and Birnbeck Island. I am fortunate to have such a run so close at foot, so to speak, for the area of sand, mud, cliffs and the low jutting headland of Woodspring Priory make a fine backdrop to one's endeavour. And at that time in the evening, the sunsets which are created by the waters of the Severn and the hills and industries of South Wales are breathtaking.

We reached the Pier in 1 hour 15 minutes, having covered a distance of about 9 miles, and entered the Old Pier Hotel for a little light refreshment. Richard made the agreed telephone call to Carol to collect us and, as we refreshed ourselves, we talked of how good it is to be athletic and healthy and how 9 or 10 miles is just about right for that time of day. As the landlord joined in from the other side of the bar, I boasted a little about what it is like to be a marathon runner.

Chapter Three

Running on the longest day of the year. First sight of the rowing machine. Queer thoughts of New York. Running on an empty stomach. How to frighten your opponent at squash. A silly football match. A morning run through the woods.

Saturday, June 20, medical. I am not sure how or why it happens, but clearly there is a medical relationship between running and catching flu.

I started running on 30 May and within a couple of days I had a cold. A few days later it had turned into influenza and I ended up on a course of antibiotics. So my training schedule, to use the term loosely, was shot away before it began. It is difficult to prepare for a marathon whilst lying in bed with an apparent temperature of 143°, drugged to the eyeballs, with only the hot water bottle for comfort.

I lay there. Delirious dreams of a fine victory in New York swept over me: a new world record, sub-4-minute miles and the adulation of the world's top runners; garlanded press conferences, the first dance of the ball in the evening with the beautiful winner of the ladies' event (or is that Wimbledon?), and the Olympics in Los Angeles as the next inevitable object-ive. My superb running gear, all bearing my monogram dis-creetly embroidered in gold — or perhaps blue would be better — and running shoes some 10 oz lighter than their nearest competitor would, of course, all be designed by me in my studio in Covent Garden.

Thus I passed my days, happy ones in retrospect, until I was signed off by the doctor and the realities of life hit me again. So today I am better and will begin to construct these dreams of immortality. I arise early — well, just before eight — dressed in my freshly laundered tracksuit smelling of twentieth-century freshness and left the house with my 'faithful dog Dora' who was over the moon at my return to the outdoor life.

It was a short run of about 3 miles just to get the old legs moving again. Out into the road and up Hill Path, a narrow, twisting lane which runs for some 200 yards up on to Banwell Hill and is just a shade off being vertical. To walk it is difficult, to run it after spending the last few days fighting for one's life swiftly brings home the foolishness of the project. My dog began his instinctive sheepdog bit as we made the hill and the fields at the top, rounding up everything that he could set his sights on. And as the only thing that moved at that time in the morning were the flies on the cowpats, that's what got rounded up.

As the path peters out and the fields open up there is a sort of flat plateau lined with broken-down stone walls and hedges and gates which may not survive another winter. Then the land rises sharply again on its way towards the woods. It is a strenuous run to make the gate at the top which leads into the woods; I always feel that I have won a moral victory when I reach it. Today I staggered up to the five bars of galvanised metal and collapsed against them, searching the air for a little oxygen. It was then that I decided to try walking and, as it was my first time out, I did not regard my cheating as a sign of defeat but rather a slight bending of the rules.

It is beautiful up on the hill, looking north over the top of Banwell and the Somerset levels to the estuary and the Brecon Beacons in the far distance, towards Cardiff and, beyond, the Rhondda valley; in the south-west, the Quantock Hills and Exmoor to the south, Crooks Peak and the end of Mendip to the south-east and the vale of Winscombe to the east: a fine panorama in the early-morning haze.

After a brisk walk through the fields, dog and I returned home for breakfast.

Sunday, June 21, 9 miles. I think summer has arrived on the longest day of the year. It has taken up until now to warm away the winter clouds. It still seems strange to me to put on a tracksuit, leave the house and feel warm before I have actually begun to move.

I left the house at 10.30 am, ran up the High Street and away from the homes which line both sides of this narrow road. Its

27

name is derived more from its topographical positioning than its usage, as it runs for exactly 1 mile along the north side of Banwell Hill. At the far end I took a left turn at the T-junction which leads up to the farm. Everywhere was colour and life that had not been there before, or perhaps I'm just more awake at 10.30 than I am at 7.30.

Down the short slope at the end of the hill I ran, across the motorway bridge and up again into Christon, a small village some 1½ miles from Banwell, along the quiet and peaceful lane that wanders between the high stone walls, capped with 'lords and ladies' as is the Somerset fashion. I was 15 minutes out and already my head was filled with thoughts of yesterday, of times long before I was around when such villages were England and not merely a fascinating reminder of what life used to be like — Thomas Hardy, training for a marathon:

I moved at a steady pace not unbecoming for one such as I on such a day, nor in order to solicit glances and disapproving nods from the inhabitants of the dispersed village with its rough undressed stone walls, many of which lack the attention due to them. But nature has a way of binding them together with deep green ivy. And where the ravages of time have dealt a permanent blow and removed huge sections she has replaced them with blackthorn and elder, honeysuckle and wisteria, wild clematis and pink dog roses. And along the side of the lane, amid the uncut grass, springs blue germander speedwell and the long tufty stakes of the white common meadow rue, periwinkles and zigzag clover with its rich purple flowers.

Besides myself, there were few intruders in Christon on that Sunday morning. Those that were there were attending matins in the Norman church, and I wondered which of us would be spiritually purer by mid-day.

As I passed the church, so I also passed the vicar, as well dressed for his part in this performance as I was for mine. But I felt a degree of guilt about performing such a pagan activity as running on the sabbath. 'Six days shalt thou labour and on the seventh thou shalt not train for a marathon.' I passed him in silence, feeling relieved at not being admonished, and promptly ran into another vicar coming the other way. Clearly the place was full of vicars and, equally clearly, no place for the likes of me. I quickened my pace and, glancing over my shoulder, observed the holy brace as they entered the church by the heavily studded oak door, letting out the muted sounds of the organ and '*Laudes Domini*'. I quitted the village faster than I had entered it and left the good people of Christon to their devotions.

The beautiful valley which lies between Christon, Loxton and Barton, surrounded and protected by gentle hills, must epitomize the English landscape. The highest of these hills is Crooks Peak, some 700 feet above sea level. For hundreds of years this enclosed vale must have provided incalculable peace and solitude for those people who lived and worked there. Just ten years ago, however, the M5, with its six lanes of black tarmac, was planted straight through the middle of it.

I felt hot and well as I ran through Loxton, turning left across the second motorway bridge. I sped past Compton Bishop, a village nestled snugly beneath the horseshoe shape of Wuthering Down, finally arriving at the home of the man who had started me off on all this. Mark had in his possession a devious device called a rowing machine which he had purloined for an article in the magazine, and as my need for such an object was greater than his, agreed to lend it to me. I accepted it gratefully, ignorantly, foolishly, rather as a mouse accepts cheese, and returned with it to Banwell by car.

Monday, June 22, 3 miles. I left the house at eight o' clock. It would seem that to run round Banwell Hill each morning during the week is a good idea. If I could do 3 miles before the clamour of the day set in, it would be something at least.

I felt tired from the exertion of the previous day and the warmth from the morning sun. Beautiful to run, though, on this, the first day of Wimbledon.

Then I suddenly thought of New York some three or four months away and a most peculiar feeling shot through my body, beginning deep inside my stomach and radiating down my arms and legs. It passed quickly but it was the first touch of panic I'd felt about the marathon.

Wynt Hill was easier this time (if that were possible), although I felt sweat pumping out of me before I reached the Pattersons' house at the bottom. It is a large mansion of a place, rebuilt in the classic English tradition around the turn of this century, a pleasant building with a tennis court and a newly built pool heated by a bank of solar panels which give the impression that one is approaching Goonhilly Downs.

At the top of the hill my recovery time was noticeably quicker than before and I was able to pick my legs up, quicken my pace and focus my eyes on the hedgerows and fields. Previous efforts in this direction resulted in blurred views and a strange thumping noise which quite startled me at first until I recognised it as my heart beat. Back at home I was even able to raise a faint smile to myself as I sat on the steps in the kitchen. I thought maybe I was getting the hang of it.

Tuesday, June 23, 3 miles. I had returned home from a 'hard day at the office' and, as is my wont, had made for the kitchen and set to with the weekend's leftovers. Before an hour was up I had prepared a fine meal for five out of the bones of Sunday's chicken with the addition of green and red peppers, mushrooms, rice, onions and egg and a stock consisting of turmeric, soy sauce, a little garlic and some barley. I decanted the apple wine from one of the many demi-johns which line the top shelf of the well-worn Welsh dresser, and was about to begin part two, that is the eating and drinking, when in walked Richard, suggesting a quick 3-miler around the hill.

Timing has never been one of his strong points and I pointed this out to him as I left the house with the sight of my family tucking into my meal and the vision of my plateful drying out in the bottom oven of the Aga. But around the hill we went again and, what with the moaning about the 'hard day' and the grumbling about how hungry I was and how you should never run on an empty stomach, the time passed quickly.

Wednesday, June 24, 3 miles. Now about the rowing machine. It is a fine white structure similar in appearance to a fireguard; an

Hibachi barbecue with a set of shock absorbers fixed to the side. To work it, one sits on a sliding plastic seat and inserts one's feet through a set of restraining nylon straps, by which some indication is given of the horrors to come. (I mean, if you need to be strapped down to do anything it implies that something unnatural is about to happen.) You place both hands on the handles, legs bent in front of you in the classic 'in' position and then, with a great push on the legs and a pull with the arms and a loud hiss from the shock absorbers, you are able to create the sensation of pain all over your body without actually going anywhere.

How wonderful, I thought. I wondered why nobody had thought of such a contraption before. Everyone should have one; an ideal Christmas present for Granny. Whether or not it would actually do me any good, only time would tell. To date, with a total usage of about 15 minutes, my thoughts were that anything that could create that much discomfort in such a short period of time must be rearranging the metabolism somehow.

I soon began really to hate that machine. If you are playing squash or tennis, there is always the other person to swear at and loathe, and if that doesn't seem to be working you can always destroy a racquet or two. If things get really bad you can even walk off the court and refuse to have anything further to do with your opponent. But try any of these with a rowing machine and see where it gets you. It is a despicable object. It is constructed so as to be indestructible, and should you ever reach a point where you think that you have the better of it, it clicks into another gear and you're back where you started. A rowing machine is something that no self-respecting secret police force should ever dream of being without, something they could drag up from the cellar when the water torture and the electric shock treatment had failed to deliver the goodies from some poor wretch who could not get his cyanide pills down himself quick enough. Three minutes on the rowing machine and none of the world's secrets would be safe.

From now on I decided to call it Nora (short for Bloody Nora). I had resolved to punish myself on Nora for a few minutes before each run and there was to be no exception on this warm, delicate, summer day. But I was tired: I had just watched two exhausting hours of Wimbledon on television and, not wishing to overdo it, had decided to take a steady trot around the hill.

Up the High Street I went and along the road, between the neatly positioned assortment of old and new houses, the flip-flop of my running shoes echoed by the plip-plop of the tennis floating out of the open windows. I experienced no real problems, just a great deal of sweat on this most humid day of the year to date. And my time of 27 minutes was only 2-3 minutes slower than when I really tried to push myself. I did find that strange.

Friday, June 26, 3 miles. I had a squash match at six o' clock in the evening and the court, 3 miles away, seemed about the correct distance for a swift run. If nothing else, the horror in the mind of my opponent that he was about to play someone who was so fit that he could sprint the 3 miles to the club and then play a 40-minute session of squash should have the desired effect and give me a fine victory.

It took me 22 minutes to cover the fairly flat course and parts were even enjoyable. Some sections, along the main Sandford-to-Banwell road, were most unpleasant as cars and trucks thrashed past at 60 mph within a foot or two of my foot or two.

There was time for a 10-minute break before the game. And it certainly worked, this wicked false impression which I had hoped to cause; this delightful delusion. To my glee, the effect was heightened by the behaviour of the receptionist, who insisted on telling all around that I was a marathon runner, that I had just run from Banwell to play a game of squash and how extraordinarily fit I must be and how impressed she was and that she would tell her overweight husband about it and see if it would 'get 'im outa the pub an' lose some o' that fat belly what he has'.

Sunday, June 28. The Banwell School Parents' Association held their crazy football competition for a couple of hours in the morning. Our team of five went as the Avon Schools

Maintenance Service under our banner proclaiming 'We have never knowingly overworked'. God knows how everybody else felt at the end but I felt good and knackered after running around dressed up as a charlady and carrying a mop and bucket. The beer tasted sweet, however, as we drank from the winners' silver cup in the Bell at lunchtime.

Thursday, July 2, 2 miles. Up over the hill early in the morning. A long struggle to the top of the open field and a scramble over the gate and on into the woods, all thick with ivy and brambles, almost hiding the narrow path that runs through its centre. The nettles on the open ground were so tall that they had begun to lose control and flop lazily across the path, turning my normal regular stride into a slow, staggered step, with an occasional rude word as I failed to negotiate the more protruding of these virulent plants.

Through the cool wood I ran with my dog, who runs twice as quickly and covers twice the distance, following the scent of fox or badger. Sometimes he would disappear from sight to reappear 50 yards ahead and run back towards me with a grin on his face and an effortless stride as I puffed and panted. Bloody dog. Why doesn't he do the marathon and I'll lie in the garden chewing bones with dreams of hunting wild rabbits?

I walked down Hill Path on the way back. It really is steep and running down it is asking for all sorts of trouble.

Chapter Four

How can an athlete reconcile normal everyday life with high aspirations? An awful run down Riverside. A cricket match at Lower Langford. Training continues in London. The sad consequences of a sojourn in the capital.

Saturday, July 4, 6 miles. Today I needed to run fast. After a blistering day at college on Friday I had been able to manage only a long walk. Moreover, it had been playing on my mind for a while that I had been more than a little dozy about my speed over 5 or 6 miles. I had begun to get myself into a rhythm which had become far too comfortable to be doing me much good. There was a real need to push myself harder.

So off down Riverside I went, but instead of employing my usual ambling stride I started to lift my legs and push off with my toes. The difference was quite staggering. I soon discovered that my concentration had to be much greater than if I had just been trotting along. I found it difficult to notice what was going on around. My eyes began to get firmly fixed on a patch of stony road some 5 yards in front of me, and soon the continual blurred pattern of moving road had me mesmerized. I would run like this to the Weston road, a distance of 3 miles. And, having set that as some sort of target it would be pointless for me not to do it, or cheat and settle for 1½ miles instead.

At last I felt as I imagined a real runner feels in training. I had just joined Westbury Harriers, partly because I had to in order to compete in New York and partly because real committed runners like Dave Frances and Jerry and Shirley Smith were there and at least I would know someone if I decided to take up track events at some time in the future. Perhaps I was becoming an athlete, running quickly, breathing deeply, concentrating hard, wearing the proper gear and the inevitable serious expression. Me, my, whoever would have thought it: Rob Burn, marathon runner. I wonder when the next Commonwealth Games are?

A large blue-grey heron rose into the air from out of one of the smaller rhines which feed the river. A huge, clumsy bird that seems to object to having to lift its unwieldy bulk into the air and disapproves of any human being that gets within a hundred yards of it, the heron set off across the flat, scruffy fields in search of a little peace and quiet and a frog or two.

An extremely grumpy-looking farmer watched me pass from the top of his old grey Massey Ferguson as he took a break from haymaking. His face bore the look of a man who could not, for the life of him, see why any sane person would want to spend a warm summer afternoon 'prancin' up and down lik' a gurt fairy, daft bugger'.

I covered the 3 miles faster than I had done it before and was most satisfied with my achievement. I walked for ½ mile to regain a little breath and then ran back at my normal speed, along the wide grass bank at Black Lock, following the quiet effortless river back to Banwell. This time I was much more aware of the water and the mosquitoes and the odd plonk of a stickleback as it munched its way through an unfortunate fly, disturbing the flat surface of the river as it did so. But apart from that, the water hardly seemed to exist as on that still morning it showed nothing of itself, only the reflections of the white clouds in the blue sky.

The whole journey took about one hour and I enjoyed it tremendously. I stopped off at the Bell when I reached Banwell for a pint of orange and sodawater, kindly bought by Ivor the landlord who professed that if I was daft enough to run in the New York Marathon, he was daft enough to 'buy us a pint'.

Sunday, July 5, 2 miles. I woke late on Sunday with a terrible hangover. I had been to a wedding reception the previous afternoon where the champagne flowed, as did the sympathy for Borg who was soundly beaten by McEnroe during the Wimbledon final. I had found a lounge with a telly and a few other tennis fans and as we watched we drank and ate strawberries and cream and agreed that this was the only way in which one should ever watch the game. In the evening I had attended a birthday party at a friend's house in the village. So my cocktail for the day had been beer, white wine, champagne, home-made beer, white wine, red wine and copious quantities of port.

As I rose carefully from my bed I realised that the afore-mentioned cocktail, plus the superb food which had accompanied it, would see the light of day for the second time in fifteen hours if I did so much as move my head too quickly, let alone attempt to run round the hill. But by midday my conscience was nagging me, along with my daughter Becky, who wanted a bike ride and me for company. So I set off, running at a brisk walking pace with her following along behind, drawing level at times and saying how easy I made running look and how proud she was of me and all the time I kept a lookout for likely places to throw up without causing too much disarrangement of the landscape.

We walked together up Wynt Hill and I pointed out wild flowers to Becky and pretended that that was why I wasn't running.

'I'll ride if you want to run,' she said, but I replied that I thought it a shame not to look at the flora.

My ability to lie to my children sometimes worries me. They believe me to be of such good standing and possessing the highest morals. One day they will find out what their father is really like and their faith in human beings will be destroyed forever. The two girls will probably refuse to get married and Tom will turn gay and take up tap dancing. And it will be all my fault, all down to the fibs and fabrications constructed on such a day as this when I convinced my dear daughter that I was giving up my tight training schedule in order to instruct her on the delights of the ox-eye daisy and the red campion.

When I reached home I committed myself to 10 minutes on Bloody Nora as a penance and so felt both mentally ill at ease and physically sick as a parrot.

Tuesday, July 7, 8 miles. It is difficult to reconcile normal, ordinary everyday life with its ups, downs and pitfalls with one's pretensions as a runner. For instance, last night Richard and Carol kindly invited my wife Pat and me down to take *moules marinières* with them. The mussels had been freshly gathered at a little place called Cawsand in Cornwall whence they had just returned from a week-end's camping. After several bowlfuls of this delicious fare, washed down with one or two assorted bottles of wine, I retired for the night at some minutes past midnight.

This morning, however, things looked different. After my boasting about my successful run of the previous day, about how fast I could now move along the byways of Somerset, I now had to grovel out of bed with a wretched headache and a stomach like an organgrinder's jock strap and make for the clearer air of the great outdoors.

I ran 7 or 8 miles and it was awful. Every step of the way was sheer purgatory, all along those quiet lanes, passing the river and the green fields which only a few days before had given me so much pleasure and joy. Today even the cows which quickly lined up along the nearest hedge to watch me pass could not quite believe what a mess they saw before them. The smell of garlic moved several of them further into the centre of the field and the one or two who remained, obviously suffering from a nasal 'condition', seemed to be saying, 'Who's been a naughty boy then? Won't do that again in a hurry, will you?' And all along the route rabbits and birds brought out their young to point out the depths to which human beings can stoop and let that be a lesson to them, not to be quickly forgotten, and then led them away weeping and frightened.

I cannot remember sweating so much. I had often run in my sweatsuit with the usual shorts and T-shirt underneath, but never had the stuff poured out of me in this quantity. Within 15 minutes I was in danger of drowning, and within half an hour in danger of flooding the Somerset levels. A passing milkherd took his cows to higher ground and several small boys began hurriedly to knock up some form of raft upon which their families and favourite pets were being carefully put on board.

As I lay in my hot bath afterwards it was noticeable that my body was actually soaking up the soapy suds — positively inhaling the stuff. How do people ever live a normal, day-today, take-it-as-it-comes, commonplace life and train to be marathon runners at the same time?

Wednesday, July 8. The cricket match at Langford, the Gentlemen's Squash XI versus an All Comers XI from the University of Bristol Veterinary School, was played on a glorious evening within earshot of the village clock, which duly struck the quarter, half, three-quarter, and hour as it had obviously done since time, as we know it, had begun. The newly painted wooden clapboard pavilion provided both changing-room facilities and an electric kettle for cups of tea. The ladies and friends of the cricket club rested lazily against the rickety balustrade with its well-worn boardwalk or lay in the shade of the large scoreboard which constantly recorded the progress of the two teams. It did not do this correctly, but then that is not necessarily the point of such an object: it is there rather to tell those out on the field that there is still someone awake or even alive, back beyond the boundary line.

It was a beautiful day with the wicket playing well and true. Fine puffs of chalky white dust flew up as the ball and bat met on a full-pitched delivery. The result of this limited-over match, although never in doubt for one moment, was a fine victory for the Gentlemen by a 4 being hit by our captain off the penultimate ball of our innings. There was of course the sprinkle of applause from the spectators and players as is the custom, and after hurriedly stuffing the implements into a well-worn brown leather bag, all parties retired to the Crown for a pleasant drink and to debate the various decisions which the assortment of umpires had made during the three or so hours of the match.

As for me, I simply told the blind bat who gave me out to an LBW decision when I was on 16 and just beginning to get my eye in that if I ever caught him on a dark night within the next five years, I'd remove his googlies.

Thursday, July 9, 3 miles. A quick 3 miles before friends arrived for a meal in the evening. I had been grafting in my cellar doing finicky artwork: the usual head down, scalpel in hand, surgically preparing the type and illustration for print. The only enjoyable part was when Lucy came down and began drawing flowers from the garden on to a large sheet of white paper. She is beautiful and I do so hope that she carries on with her drawing and painting.

But then to rush out into the roads and fly like the wind (well, not exactly, but it doesn't hurt to overstate the case now and again) without any preparation or forethought can be fatal, so I took the hill at a fairly slow pace and made it in 25 minutes which was faster than I thought I had done it. Wynt Hill, that recurring 'boil on the bum', rendered its familiar pain on my body. What it has against me I really don't know as I've never done it any harm, but I swear that it has enough pent-up hatred to last a lifetime.

Friday, July 10. Today I travelled to London to do two days of freelance graphics for ITN as part of the coverage of the recent spate of riots. I knew for a fact that this was going to present another set of problems, the old mind-over-matter bit. I packed my running gear, more as a gesture than anything else, at the bottom of my hold-all, just in case. But what were the chances of a good run? I'd never left ITN sober yet.

Saturday. It's so difficult to think about running when you're stuck in a design studio, a bar, a pub or a restaurant. Oh how easily I slide back into those evil habits, so well cultivated through years of enjoyment.

Sunday. This morning I'm not working. So I rise from my bed about ten o' clock and after three fine cups of tea, drunk to retain consciousness, I run up to Clapham Common. The common is about ½ mile away from the house where I usually stay when I graft in London. The last time I did this particular trek around the park was the day before the London Marathon some six months before and as I catch sight of the green open space from Taybridge Road, the memories come flooding back of that cold spring morning and my lonely circuit with only the butterflies and fear for company.

Today, however, it is warm and sunny and the common is full of people walking dogs, playing football or cricket irrespective of season, or fishing around the circular pond on the south side. The run is a great deal less emotional than the last one and after a couple of days in smoky London Town I feel quite at home in my running gear. The puffing, panting and breathlessness are like old friends as I speed past families, dogs, cats and kids on bikes and feel reassured about the future after the futility of the riots which have sprung up all over the country. I return for a hot bath and grapefruit juice in huge greedy quantities, scrambled eggs on toast and lashings of tea.

Monday, July 14, 6 miles. As I left London behind, so I also left its values; its good time, its late nights, its lack of sleep. I think it is the last which destroys me more than the others. The jumbos begin their descent into Heathrow about six o'clock in the morning, having travelled halfway round the world in the same space of time that it takes for the beer drunk the night before to turn itself into a hangover. And at six in the morning I could swear that they are doing it on purpose or that they fly through one ear and out of the other.

Since starting training I had become aware of scales, the bathroom sort which seldom record the same weight but do give some indication as to whether one should feel optimistic or pessimistic. I find on average that one day in London equals about 3 lb in fat, a strange equation which may be expressed as

$$\frac{1 \times 24 \text{ hrs} \times \text{Lon}}{48 \text{ oz}} = \text{bulk}.$$

I had noticed that, generally speaking, I was going in the right direction, but I was also aware that I was getting a bit paranoid about the whole thing. I'd never really cared before, and suddenly I was beginning to nurse myself rather like one might care for an ailing azalea. I was dismayed to discover, therefore, that after my short stay in London I was 7 lb heavier than before and I resented the idea of having to run it all off. The best I could do was a slow jaunt around the hill, preceded by Becky on her bike.

Training did not seem to be going well. There were always so many other things to do and I had only been out twice during the past week. If I didn't improve radically I wouldn't even be fit enough for a pensioners' 'fun run' in 2002. I really felt bad at times about what needed to be done and the fact that I was not doing it. All the crooning of a couple of weeks before about how good I felt and it was 'off to the pub for a pint of Guinness' had evaporated. I felt tired and wretched and I still was not sleeping properly.

I had rejected the idea of going out for a second run today. I just could not be bothered. I didn't even have the energy to debate it with myself, I just rejected it out of hand and would have been content to sit and watch the early evening telly had not Richard wandered in, suitably attired for a jog.

I changed reluctantly and we agreed to run around the hill but in the opposite direction. This I had not done since the beginning of January and it evoked memories of one of my first attempts to run 3 miles. It had been still within the twelve days of Christmas and it felt as if I had been pulling the 26 lb turkey, a plum pudding and a crate or two of beer behind me. This time it was easier and the comparison gave me a little extra heart.

Running down Wynt Hill was rather like waving two fingers at someone who had been annoying you for months. God, how I enjoyed that part. The effortless running. The laughing instead of the panting. And at a point where normally I resorted to filthy language, today I managed an extra turn of speed and a swagger.

There is always a dark side to life, however, and Wynt Hill is no exception. Smile whilst you can, for the next bend will produce something unpleasant. What goes down must go up. I suppose it is logical that if one starts and finishes a run at the same point, the amount of 'uphill' is equal to the total amount of 'downhill'. The way out of this sort of thinking is obvious, though. All I need to do is to run about ten times the distance each week!

Chapter Five

Guilt and remorse induce a near-suicidal run to the Old Pier. My first blister. Self-doubt and uncertainty. A new positive attitude is called for. The possibility of making a film is raised.

Sunday, July 19, 8 miles. I had been away in London again for the weekend, up with the family to stay with friends, and what a lovely time we all had had, eating lashings of well-prepared food and tasting a fine selection of local brews. I returned home late on Sunday. Realising that I had been a little slack of late, I resolved to do a quick, short run just to show willing. So I changed and, as the scales were close at foot, I leapt on them with a clear conscience. '12 bloody stone, 2 bloody pounds!' Over ½ a bloody stone heavier than I had been one and a half weeks before!

This was dreadful. How could I possibly put on ½ stone just like that? I gazed down at my extended stomach, rushed to the full-length mirror on the landing for some little comfort or small reassurance. But I got none. Everything I saw in the mirror was me. Oh help! If every time I stopped running for a day or two, or talked to a friend, or got into my motor car I put on so much weight, what on earth was going to happen to me?

I resolved to run every day ... for ever ... 'I'll show you, you fat podge, who has the self-control ... don't think you can get the better of me ... fatty ... fatty ... you weak-willed, pathetic excuse for a runner.'

I hurriedly threw on a load of running kit — anything, it didn't really matter. I rushed downstairs, through the kitchen, shouting something rude to Pat who asked if I was going to help her with the unpacking. I ran out of the house and into the oppressive evening.

Where to? Where can I lose ½ stone on a Sunday night? Everywhere's closed! Down Riverside. I could feel all the consequences of the weekend's enjoyment swelling up inside me, along with the guilt. I kept wanting to stop. I felt so ill. But it had become a mental thing — mind over excess matter! Brain over brawn (boiled gammon actually)! — and I somehow managed to keep on running.

After 2 miles I resolved to run to the Old Pier although the thought of running 8 or 9 miles in my condition had a certain death wish to it — Billy Bunter doing the 100 metres, cream buns and all. I did manage to get into some sort of rhythm but it was painful, my stomach leading the way through the evening air and Kewstoke Woods. I reached the pier, however, feeling that I had resolved not to give up the struggle without a fight. Then I phoned Pat who reluctantly came out to fetch me.

I am not really sure if that was such a good thing to have done, in retrospect. Normally I would never run on such a fat stomach, especially after such a period of inactivity. But I did need some sort of jolt to make me realise that there was no way in which I could reconcile these two extremes of life. I had to begin to think seriously about giving up some of life's pleasurable things in order to attain some degree of fitness. I slept badly that night, thinking about running and working, but I had at least run off 3 lb.

Monday, July 20, 4 miles. A bit of a mixture today. Two hours of tennis with a friend, Steve, at Clevedon, followed by a 4-mile run along the sea front. Over Wains Hill, a sort of high headland that juts out to the south of Clevedon and then along the sea wall that extends some 5 miles down the coast, separating the mud flats from the reclaimed farmland leading to Kingston Seymour.

I had lived nearby several years before and much of the landscape was familiar: the thick grey mud of the Severn estuary with its watery ditches, like witches' fingers, draining the water back from the land and out to the muddy sea; the gulls and peewits, still fighting over some luckless lugworm out on the flats. It's wonderful out there — nothing to hear but the sounds of the birds and the sea.

Once back at Steve's house I indulged again in the wine and the food of a good night out, but as I had had a fair quantity of exercise for an aperitif I did not feel too guilty. This guilt feeling is quite strange: I have noticed that it is becoming the norm to have it as a companion. Things always seem fine until the next morning and then all the horrors, fears, regrets and doubts begin. 'Oh, what have I done?... how could I?... will I ever be the same again?... will I go blind?... deaf?... limp, or even worse? I will never do that again. I promise to be good from now on. If God forgives ... just this one last time.'

The trouble is, however, that I'm thirty-six. All these feelings of guilt are associated with adolescence, not 'rapidly approaching' or approached middle age. Why should I feel like this? Every morning I look back at how many cigars I smoked yesterday, how many pints of beer I downed — such simple pleasures and nothing to feel bad about. Surely I am being totally unreasonable to myself, unfair, too critical by half? I have done nothing to be so ashamed of.

But I will try and be good, oh Lord, if you get me around New York in 3 hours 30 minutes.

Wednesday, July 22, 18 miles. I had been working at home today and I had a feeling that something nasty was about to happen, that something evil was beginning to fester. At about 5.30 I set off up the High Street, wondering where my wandering feet would take me.

I sometimes think that my brains are in my feet, although I do have every confidence in them to make the correct decisions. They occasionally play nasty tricks on the rest of me, the little scamps, but generally they are as reliable as the Bank of England. Today I could watch them from some 2 metres above as they pondered the whys and wherefores of the various options open to them. I thought it best to keep out of the conversation, although I did offer a couple of points for consideration: (1) I wasn't very fit and (2) dinner would be ready in about three-quarters of an hour. Perhaps they could bear that in mind before coming to a final solution. But feet can be as bloody-minded as the rest of one and today mine chose to ignore both points.

Off we went, therefore, all three of us, to Hutton and Uphill, some 6 or 7 miles, meeting the blustery beach some 50 minutes later. I was running in my shorts and T-shirt and I felt reasonably good. It was windy but dry. From the wide expanse of sands at Uphill the views of Wales were splendid, finely etched and giving the illusion of nearness. Even from Banwell I had noticed how clear the hills of Brean Down and Kewstoke were and had fallen for this old illusion hook, line and sinker. I should have known better, a man of my experience, but I think that the brief discord with my feet had distracted me somewhat and I therefore blame the decision to try to run around the top end of Avon firmly on them.

'It is only across to that hill', or 'it's just around that bend' are all very well, but the reality is that to run 'just around that hill' is a heck of a long way. On a day when the rain is coming down or the sea mists are covering the beaches and undercliffs and the clouds shroud the tops of the hills, there is a tendency to have a much greater respect for the task in hand. On this clear day, however, it was only when I reached the beach that I realised that my feet had committed me to an 18-miler.

By the middle of the sands I had been running for about an hour. The further I ran, the more insular I became, finding it difficult to notice what was going on outside my head. Now and again my feet would land in soft sand, that strange sinking feeling after the hardness and the uncompromising regularity of the road: kicking sand and flattening worm casts, running just above the receding waterline.

Another 3 miles and I was at the Old Pier. I was beginning to feel weary after the 10-mile mark and my strides were noticeably shorter, but I felt better than I could remember feeling on a comparative trip out during my training for the London Marathon back in March.

Through Kewstoke Woods I persevered, the incoming tide on my left splashing noisily, relentlessly against the rocks below me. At Worle I began to feel my first blisters. I had never had blisters during training and I wondered why I was beginning to get them now. Wondering why I should get them naturally did not lessen the fact that I had them and that they were hurting like hell and the thought of another 5 or 6 miles seemed most unpleasant.

As I left the built-up streets of Worle and St George's I felt tired and heavy-legged, unable to think about anything else other than the task of keeping one leg in front of the other; and my old friend 'General Fatigue' accompanied me for the rest of the journey. The ½ mile up through Church Street and then the High Street was really difficult and the desire to slow to a walk for the last few hundred yards overwhelming, as if it would not have been possible to run any further if there had been an extra mile to go. Knowing that you are about to stop running and wanting to stop creates a most peculiar sensation within you. You just wind yourself up to a point which you can see in front of you, and when you reach it, it's all over. I had run 18 miles. How could I possibly keep going for another 8? God! Another 8 on top of that!

The kitchen clock showed that I had taken 2 hours 25 minutes, and I flopped down on the steps. Suddenly I began to feel sick. I rushed past the family who had eaten long ago and were now in the middle of a card game.

'I've just done 18 miles,' I said without looking at them.

'Your dinner will be bloody awful by now, then,' blurted back Pat without looking at me.

I reached the bathroom, sat on the loo and buried my head in my knees for a good 5 minutes before finding enough strength of character to stand up and run a bath. I was not sick but I had never felt as bad as that after a long run. Thoughts of 18 miles equals 2 hours 25, therefore 26 miles equals ... and I managed to work it out at about 3 hours 35. But that was ridiculous, because the idea of carrying on for another 8 miles at any speed at all, let alone at the same as the previous 18, was out of the question.

I plopped into the hot bath filled to the top and pondered. I felt bewildered, confused about the whole thing. What was possible and what was not? Blisters on both feet, feeling sick after the run. Am I getting worse or simply not as fit as I think I should be? I just lay there and could not work it out.

Friday, July 24. The lingering weakness which I had had during the last couple of days was still with me. I certainly could not have done anything yesterday but resolved to attempt a 3-miler today. It's strange how a long run really knocks the stuffing out of you.

So even with the old pins still very much asleep, I managed to push them out of the house and up Hill Path towards the woods at the top. But my victory was short-lived. It lasted some 3 minutes and some 300 yards and there it turned into a nasty defeat.

Half way up Hill Path the legs stopped and refused to move any more and no amount of argument or reasoning could convince them otherwise. 'Come on, old things, not much further to the top,' I coaxed, although it clearly was and they knew it as well as the rest of me did and such shallow deceit never fooled anybody. 'Once there, it will be on the level, and then downhill all the way back, and it's only a couple of miles you're trying to do and you did do 18 miles yesterday and you are not going to be beaten by a piddling little hill are you? Surely not?'

My legs took on a stubborn, strangely quiet, determined stance, conferred with the rest of me and declared a general strike. The old management-versus-labour confrontation: 'All out, brothers.' I stood there looking down at my poor tired pins. 'There is a refusal at Hill Path. "Knackered Legs" out of "What the Hell" and sired by "General Fatigue" has refused at Hill Path.'

I then had a bright idea. Today I would cheat. I would pretend that the only reason I was there was to inspect the course for next week's 'Under Tens' race which I had been asked to organise. That way I could pretend that I had no intention of actually running anywhere today and so through subtle subterfuge and cunning, salvage a little face from such a humiliating defeat. Yes, that was a good idea and anyway it needed to be done and I couldn't keep putting it off like this, day after day. So I would do it now and get it over with, and to ensure that it was done properly I would walk it slowly, very slowly. So I progressed, pitifully, up to the top of Banwell Hill along the lanes of excuses and compromise.

Saturday, July 25, 5 miles. Up and out! A new positive attitude: that was what was called for. Yesterday I would forget — it was just a temporary setback, nothing to concern myself about; an attack of weakness, brought on by overtiredness and lack of moral fibre. I would certainly see that it did not happen again.

I decided to run along the High Street, past the farm, over the first bridge and on upwards into Christon Woods. It was a good day: not so much because of the weather, which showed a total misunderstanding of which season it was, but internally I felt better.

Soon after leaving the High Street the lane turns into a sort of stoney track which leads into pine woods. The track is wide enough to get a Land Rover or tractor up but certainly it would be inadvisable to attempt the same in a car owing to the roughness of the road. So it was painful underfoot, weaving from one side of the track to the other, focusing on the ground some yard or two ahead to search out a suitable spot to land. From side to side I passed, avoiding first the stones and then the mud and then the holes. It was a slow, painful trek upwards and the lane had no intention of making life easier for me. It took me 15 minutes to reach a flatter, more friendly patch.

The sounds of the motorway passed quickly as I entered the woods and the small dips or valleys which form these hills. It was silent apart from the startled blackbirds objecting to my intrusion, which was an ungainly one as I grunted and spluttered into their midst after the incline, and fat podgy wood pigeons moving almost vertically through the coniferous trees. Further on, where the rough path begins to turn into a country lane, there was only the sound of my running shoes on the tarmac, echoing, bouncing and rebounding off the small stone cottages and woodlands. Way in front a startled horse pricked up its ears and began moving awkwardly, long before its rider was aware that there was a runner moving up on him.

What a beautiful place to be. Oh! that such places were not so rare!

Monday, July 27, 6 miles. Today I received a box of goodies from the sports magazine: tracksuits, shoes, T-shirts, sweatshirts and some sort of all-weather top. There was two of everything, just like Noah's Ark. Maybe they are going to mate! How remarkable to get given so many presents when it isn't even Christmas. I spent the day in and out of the various items and decided that I looked like a right tart and enjoyed every minute of it.

I called Richard late, about nine o'clock, and we decided to take a run down Riverside, stopping beyond Bow Bridge to navigate the resident family of swans who had taken up a position half on the grassy bank and half on the road. My training companion was feeling thoroughly disgusted at the injustices of life in general and spent several minutes of our run past the slowly flowing river supporting the role of the proletariat in modern society while I took on the role of the middle-class privileged element and found it to my liking. D. H. Lawrence was right when he said that we should do away with the working classes and all become aristocrats.

Apart from the late supper which I had recently had and at one time I thought I was about to have again, I enjoyed the run. It was a quiet, still night, and as we returned to Banwell back along Riverside all was quiet and peaceful. The swan family had turned in for the night and the lights of the Brewer's Arms shone out in the darkness.

Tuesday, July 28. A strange thing happened today. Some time ago, way back when all this malarky began, I had spoken with Nick Shipley, a film and telly man who labours both at the college and under his own steam, about the possibility of making a film about the New York Marathon. The idea was to monitor the progress of one man, namely me, who was not a runner of any standing, as he prepared for the ordeal and then, of course, follow him around the roads of New York on the big day. It would be based on the writing which I would by then have done.

Well, Nick wrote this atrocious shooting script which, owing to its high content of sentiment and romance, could easily have been mistaken for an episode of 'The Waltons' and sent it off to the BBC. Neither of us thought a great deal about it as we had heard nothing during the past month but to our alarm there was now a possibility that they might take us up on it. So tonight Nick was bringing out a producer called Paul Smith to chat about it and we were to meet on Banwell Hill at 8.30 after the children's races.

In between graphics and phone calls and cooking I spent a good deal of time organising the route for the so-called mini-marathon, placing the marker flags along the 2-mile route up over the hill and through the woods. After the ceremonial lighting of the bonfire, Banwell's answer to the street parties which were being held all over the country to mark the Royal Wedding, I rounded up the hordes of under-5s for a 200-yard marathon, and the under-9s for a 'horrible, rush-along-the-flat-patch-and-then-up-the-hills marathon'. I think if the Olympics had names like that the whole thing would be much more fun: 'Today there was a new world record in the "440 yards' rush down the back straight, then out into the road and left a bit and back into the stadium, minding the blokes who are throwing the metal thing into the air, and last one home's a sissy" event.'

In all of these events I had to lead the way, which had not been my intention, and then had to carry the last little mite back to the start. And the boys went off with such haste that it took all my skills to keep up with them. Finally there was the all-comers event in which some forty kids and six adults took part — or should I say forty-six kids? It was a great success. Nobody got lost or did anything too serious to themselves. Becky came fifth, Lucy seventh and Pat tenth and I came in last, carrying the marker poles.

Towards the end of the celebrations Nick and Paul arrived, Paul puffing and panting after the climb to the top of Hill Path. 'Yes, it is a bit steep,' I said. 'I usually run it.' Nice to get one in so early, I thought. We went to the Bell and talked movie talk. It was exciting to think that if this actually got off the ground I might become famous.

Chapter Six

A repeat of the London trip. The horrors of the Leicestershire Lawn Tennis Championships. Damage to mind and body.

Wednesday, July 29, 2 miles. The day of the Royal Wedding. And me? I find myself on a train at seven o'clock in the morning on the way to London and ITN. Today I will not drink or smoke or abuse myself in any way. Wedding or not, I shall respect myself, work hard and prepare my body for the tasks at hand: the running, the writing, the filming.

By two in the afternoon I was legless. It seemed that ITN was the only place in London where people were still working as the streets around the centre were empty, and as most of the work had been done on the previous days, the normally 'hard-working' folks of ITN found their way to the bar around noon to watch the wedding on telly. And I, not wishing to appear a blackleg in this strongly unionised house, joined them. What a friendly lot they are.

During the evening, with the Goodyear blimp floating around the GPO Tower, carrying its electronic message of 'Loyal Greetings' in the dark night sky, I again took advantage of the free drinks in the bar, kindly donated by the management as a gesture of thanks.

The following morning, I did my penance — around Clapham Common; just me, my headache and my remorse.

Friday, July 31, 3 miles. The last day of ITN was less hectic than the others. I had been to, or rather caught the end of, a champagne party the night before so I was in delicate health as I did a 3-mile run before breakfast. Once back at the house I received praise and glory from my hosts for my firmness and resolve at getting up early to run despite the fact that I had a full day's work ahead of me.

So I had survived. Moreover I had retained a little pride and I left London feeling that it could have been a great deal worse.

From there I went to Leicester for a week's holiday with Mum and Dad and another attempt at the Leicestershire Tennis Championships.

Saturday, August 1. There are, I find, great similarities between the problems of surviving the Leicestershire tennis week and working at ITN. They are both amazingly difficult to get through. I meet old friends. It's good to see them fit and well, having pursued their respective paths of excellence from childhood through to ongoing middle age, and beyond.

So we play a little tennis and have a drink in the bar, more to catch up on the events of the past year than for any other reason, perhaps enjoy a meal or two in some indigenous Indian restaurant, and thus we pass the idle days of summer. From my health's point of view, the least said about the week the better. Enough to say that it would undoubtedly have been better had it never happened; better had I been ill, gravely. A mild touch of plague, possibly, for a week. Better had I suffered a broken back, even been put inside for a week for indecent exposure and then suffered the consequences and the abuse which would have surely followed. Any one of the twelve great pestilences of Egypt would have been kinder to my metabolism than the Leicestershire Lawn Tennis Week.

Daily I was subjected to damage, both on and off the court. My shoulder, now fully recovered from an argument with a rugby full back some ten months before, returned to bid me good-day and, having returned, stayed unwelcomed for the full duration. Obviously, trying to peel the skin off a tennis ball with a blunt tennis racquet induced it to return, and as it felt quite at home in Leicester, there it stayed.

I ached all over, which was incomprehensible to me. What had happened to all those muscles that I had been cultivating over the last few months by playing squash and running hundreds of miles over hill and dale? Surely there must be one or two which you use when you play tennis?

Then there were the blisters, hundreds of them, erupting all over my feet and hands. I felt like Job every time I walked on to the court.

And inside me — what on earth was going on inside my poor digestive system?

'Hello Bobby. Have a pint?'

'No thanks, James, not just now. I'm in training for the New York Marathon in October.'

'Loads of time for training, miles away. What is it, bitter?'

'Oh, all right, just a half.'

'Two pints of bitter, barman, please.'

Day in, day out it went on — and the food: curry upon curry, chilli peppers and tandooris, one after the other on the trot (and that about sums it up). My stomach fought back bravely against this guerrilla warfare which the Leicestershire Tennis Team had declared upon it. I ate and drank ferociously, as if there were no tomorrow. It felt like second nature to me to quaff three or four pints at lunchtime or plough through bacon and eggs for breakfast with lashings of fried bread.

At the end I felt as I had done before I began training for the London run. So I gave up. It was as simple as that. I resolved to enjoy every moment of my over-indulgence, get legless with a clear conscience and binge away until I was capable of bingeing no longer. But I must not be over-critical of myself. I did manage some goody points. I ran each day, not great distances but just enough to stave off any permanent damage. My schedule for the week went like this:

Monday. On my own with dog and three times round Victoria Park. Beautiful morning.

Tuesday. Feel awful. Just once round, very slowly, lest I fall over.

Wednesday. Feel appalling. Must go on, though, and do at least two circuits. I think I've left my liver in bed.

Thursday. A good run. Four times round and going fast at the end. These runs really are my salvation, even if I do feel ill sometimes.

Friday. Three times round and dog is getting the hang of it. I think he'll miss these runs and all the friends he's made when we get back home.

Saturday. Twice round, and after a night of such disgusting gluttony, very, very slowly at a pace slightly quicker than standing still.

Sunday. Three times round with a speedy last lap as a parting gesture to the park. I have really enjoyed these runs around paths so full of memories. There is so much of me still there from all those years before, and after my efforts of the last week, quite a good deal of what was left is now scattered about those green fields. God bless you, Leicestershire. I shall get round New York in spite of you, just you wait and see.

Monday, August 10, 1 mile. Reality is horrible. I don't like it at all. But I had to get the inevitable over and done with.

I changed into running gear that was smelly and damp. I had just read a small book about training and running techniques. It had gone into the effects of over-indulgences due to smoking and drinking. Whether my Aunt Paula had sent it to me with these two chapters in mind I don't know, but to read about what was happening to me was quite sobering. Certainly, according to this little runner's bible, I should have been dead yesterday, but I am still here to prove the author wrong.

The book did however contain some interesting bits on the importance of doing proper warm-up exercises and as I could see the sense in these I resolved to do them and/or a stint on Bloody Nora each day before I went out for a run. Fifty pulls on Nora, and out: up Hill Path and across the fields, up towards the woods. At the gate I stopped. I thought that to get that far had been above what I had expected, considering the previous week, so I finished off with a long walk through the woods with the dog. This was not indicative of success and I pondered on the sad state of my body, but I did believe that I had begun to think seriously about the running, and not before time. There were only thirteen weeks to go; and another of those little shivers shot through me.

Tuesday, August 11, 2 miles. Around the hill. I had been at a friend's house in the village and, being under the illusion that we were all about to eat, had just accepted a pint of beer, so putting off the prospect of a run until late afternoon. But our plans were changed and life began to get confusing as ten different people each tried to make ten different suggestions about what everybody should do, so I leapt up and rushed off into the comparative quiet outdoors.

I felt tired at first, but by the time I had travelled the mile up High Street to the farm I had found a good rhythm. The pint of ale seemed to help rather than hinder my progress and I travelled up Wynt Hill faster than I could remember doing it before. Perhaps that's the secret of Wynt Hill. All I need to do is have a pint or two before setting off. The more the better. This certainly disproves the theories in that running book.

I might survive after all.

Chapter Seven

A holiday in Porthscatho. A run on a hot day along the cliffs. Killigerran Head. A sobering sacrifice.

Wednesday, August 12. Away on holiday, camping in a small Cornish village called Porthscatho.

There are many goody points to be gained from a camping holiday and they are all to do with fitness. You are normally on your feet the entire day doing all those basic camping activities like repositioning the tent on firmer ground or away from the point at which the west wind meets the east wind which just happens to be the very spot where you have pitched your canvas. Should things go wrong, you will find that you'll also spend many of the night hours engaged in the same activity.

If you are by the sea, as we were, there is a good chance you will spend your waking hours trundling bag-loads of gear up and down cliff faces: fishing nets and rods, ice cream and sandwiches, bottles of fizzy and cans of beer. Your time will also be spent swimming and playing loony versions of cricket, rounders, football and tennis and all the other games which everybody plays on holiday and never at any other time of the year.

There is another way in which camping can keep you fit. If the nearest loo is either in the village or is represented by a 'totally secluded' uncut cornfield, usually at a distance of 1 mile, one's speed over that distance, which may be repeated several times during a single day, improves over the duration of one's stay.

Apart from these involuntary exercises, however, I did manage two superb runs during the week. The first was on the Saturday morning, around 8.30. The weather had been beautiful, very hot and dry, and leaving a run until late morning or afternoon was out of the question. During those times it was tiring enough just to sit on the beach, waddle down to the blue water and fall in.

The sun was hot in a cloudless sky as I began my run along the cliff path, early though it was. I took off my blue T-shirt and tied it round the top of my red shorts. In all the months of running I had never felt so exhilarated, so happy, so full of the richness of my environment. And all the time the clear, cool sea splashed endlessly over the grey sandstone below me and the gulls and kittiwakes circled and drifted up and down the cliff faces without care.

In one or two places the path wandered back down to the beach. One part was sandy and very soft underfoot; another was made up of large, smooth boulders which had to be negotiated at great risk if one tried to cover the ground at any sort of speed. Looking down on some unreachable cove below Killigerran Head, I was struck by the thought that there would be very little point in ever bothering to come back again from that little world where everything was so perfect that the rest of the world would be a disappointment. So I stopped at the cliff top for some 10 or 15 minutes and watched the gulls as they drifted and screamed at each other, the small inshore lobster boats as they went about minding their pots and their own business, and sat and thought about long-ago dreams which may or may not have worked. Now and again, high up, a plane would leave its white scar across the blue sky as it ferried people away from England to America or Canada. Would the same one be carrying me over there in October?

But running like this wasn't about training or conditioning or seeing how fit you can get. I had no thoughts whatsoever at that moment of getting or keeping fit; I experienced only feelings of intense joy at being so complete with what was inside and outside of my head, a deep sense of wellbeing and admiration for all that I could see around me. As the sun dried the sweat from my face and body, now and then there came a cooler breeze from off the sea and with it a fiercer sound of the sea meeting the rocks below.

During the run back, with the sun on my face, I took the lower of the two paths which were available and ran along the beach, my feet sinking several inches into the gravelly grey sand, pulling on calf muscles and forcing out sweat until it ran down my forehead and into my eyes and ears. Then back upwards I laboured to our cliff-top campsite.

I know that I'll always remember that run: the illusions, the impressions, the effect that it had on me. I'll remember it when I'm in New York. I know that when I begin to feel bad, tired, perhaps around the 18-mile mark, I'll remember this time and think on it. Secrets.

Monday, August 17, 6 miles. I repeated the cliff-top run, this time with the dog for company. Nothing seemed to have changed at all. The weather was still very hot and dry and the landmarks, although only seen once before, appeared in a familiar way. It didn't seem as far to Killigerran Head this time. Perhaps I was less absorbed in my surroundings or possibly still more than a little asleep.

I twisted my ankle slightly as I moved along the edge of the newly ploughed field. It was not a bad injury, but it was the same ankle that had been giving quite a lot of pain during the last few weeks. I passed the furthest point of my previous run by about a mile, reaching Penndennis Point, where the headland began to make its way inland. Beyond that I could see Falmouth in the distance, some 7 or 8 miles across the water. Then I began to make my way towards the road which ran parallel to the cliff-top path and, at various points along the way, moved to within a few hundred yards of it. At least the road would be kinder on my ankle for the return journey even if the view was not as good.

The dog, hot and panting, with his tongue hanging out from the side of his mouth, kept well to my side. I thought: I'm beginning to get the better of him. He must consider me quite insane, rushing around on a day such as this instead of sitting on the beach or in a nice cafe somewhere.

After running some 3 miles along the road I cut across a field, along a bridle path. The dog was well and truly beaten and plodded along behind as if on a lead; not that he'd stay that way for long but I think he was impressed, judging from the look on his face. It had been another wonderful run. I felt intense satisfaction at having done it and deep pleasure at being able to, being physically fit enough to keep going and still capable of enjoying my surroundings. I had been fortunate indeed to be able to come to such a beautiful area and take advantage of it and I wished that everybody could do that run just once in their lifetime.

Wednesday, August 19. Back home. We had stayed overnight with Mark and his wife Jane in their house in a small village just outside Exeter and had spent the entire evening eating and drinking and imagining the glories or the failures of the next few weeks. It was a good night and I really enjoyed it, but I was not enamoured of the consequences the following morning.

The drive up from Exeter was dreadful. After the exhilaration of camping and running and being well and truly away from it all, to have to come to terms with real life in the form of the M5, with my head in the state in which it was, was sobering to say the least. My attempt at a run during the evening was a failure. My body just would not move and I think it had every reason not to. I walked slowly back towards Banwell at about 8.30. The weather had turned a little. It was overcast and not as warm as the previous few days. Everything seemed pointless.

Running could be so good. It could give me so much and then I'd go out and 'enjoy' myself and afterwards couldn't even move one leg in front of the other for more than a few hundred yards. Some pathetic progress I seemed to be making ... And so, the ultimate sacrifice: should I? shouldn't I? Yes, I would.

So on Wednesday 19 August I gave up booze until after the marathon in New York, but resolved that on that day I would drink a bottle of champagne all to myself, finish or not, good or bad. In fact, I thought, should I get round in about 3.30, I'd drink two.

Part Two

from Hill Path, Bannell Hill

A competitive element appears. Indecision and thoughts of New York. The Wedmore 6-Mile Race. The Burn Condition. Nagging fears. The eternal battle between good and evil. Lethargy.

Thursday, August 20, 7 miles. Down Riverside. It seems strange looking down at brown legs on stoney roads after the hot, dusty cliff tops of Cornwall. There was a difference in my attitude to the running there: I was on holiday and had experienced a change of sync, perhaps. Here the running was about trying harder every time I went out, to see if I could finish a run faster or feel less tired at the end. Possibly I have become more competitive. It's still enjoyment, but gained in a different way.

Before venturing out I did a handful of the disgusting body contortions which my little bible recommended. The effect seemed to be that I now felt awful before I left the house as well as when I got back. Riverside looked flat and familiar, as if I'd never been away. Even the river and the overhanging willows and narrow rhines could not match the landscape of Cornwall but everything was in its own place. All beauty is comparative and it is difficult to see new beauty in somewhere so familiar.

My run took me 55 minutes for the 7 miles and, after the failure of yesterday, gave me a good deal of satisfaction, as it had been done without any undue hardship apart from my right ankle which is beginning to be a bit of a pain. I was wearing a neoprene ankle support, a trendy bit of gear which gave the illusion of helping, even if it didn't. I had covered the distance at a steady pace. For about 7 miles I could now keep the same rhythm and speed without slowing down at the end, although I was daydreaming a bit when I crossed the main Weston road and nearly ran into a car.

Saturday, August 22, 3 miles. I felt renewed. A couple of days without running and I had a strong desire to try a fast run round the hill at about ten o'clock in the morning. Although I'm reasonably awake at that time it still feels strange to do such violent exercise and then begin running. I think it took about a mile before I realised that I was in full flight — past the farm and going like a good 'un.

I felt better than for some time and took pleasure in pushing off hard with my toes. Even Wynt Hill, although still a pig, did not present any real threat to my ego. And at the top I accelerated quickly away and back home. It took me 21 minutes, the fastest time yet. My performance was due for an improvement and I should begin to take the whole thing more seriously than the London run. I wondered if it was because I was getting into the 'can I do a personal best?' attitude, or whether the film and the writing were spurring me on.

Sunday, August 23, 14 miles. I leave the house at about 1.45 and run into the High Street. Stop. Here we go again. Go on, old son, commit yourself. Perhaps my problem in life isn't the ability to finish things, to which I have always credited my desire to run marathons, but my inability to make decisions. So possibly I should get changed in the morning, rush out into the street, decide to run 15 miles, quickly and promptly, and then equally quickly forget it and walk back inside the house, have a nice bath and a cup of tea, and leave it at that. How simple and time-saving that would be.

Up it is. And my route ahead is perfected before I reach the end of the street: Banwell, Hutton, past the factory where they do things which nobody can talk about but where, I believe, they spend my hard-earned money in devising cunning new ways of destroying humanity in the name of peace, love and justice and the national economy; past the nurseries, then up the steep hill into Hutton village, a persistent entrant in the 'Britain in Bloom' competition and where each June the wall-flowers and the begonias find their way into plastic cider barrels (such is progress) to line the thin road which leads on to the sea at Uphill.

From there I ran along the Bridgwater-to-Weston road and turned off to the left to Bleadon village, some 7 miles after leaving Banwell. It was about there that my ankle began to play up again and I decided that I would once more visit my friendly physiotherapist in Bristol. It is something that I can well do without. All this training is quite hard enough without the perpetual fear that, at any time, something irreversible is about to happen to my foot.

The sun came out as I began the uphill slog out of Bleadon and the second 7 miles of my run back home. Thoughts of New York filled my head as I passed Bleadon Hill on my left, the odd farms on my right with their even odder selection of tents pitched in orchards as the summer visitors take advantage of the Somerset countryside.

New York won't be hot like this, not in October, not as the cool sea winds come off the North Atlantic. 3,500 miles away. And my mind just vanishes into an event which hasn't even taken place yet and which has no substance whatsoever and yet how real it all feels. The tall buildings, the Verrazano Narrows Bridge and the starting line; Central Park and the people whooping it up as we run through their streets and the times when I shall feel really bad and then afterwards, if things work out well, how good it will all be.

But what if I go too quickly, blow up after about 18 miles? Or too slow and potter in, in about 4½ hours, all healthy and disappointed and slower than in London? But then I suppose that, having done all this training and the London Marathon, I should have a fairly clear idea about how fast or slow to run. At least I have a little advantage over those who have never run this kind of race before.

Thus absorbed, I finished my run in good time — about 1.45 for 14 miles. If I carried that speed all the way, for the full 26, it would make a 'sub-3.30', as they say in the running trade. Hell, I don't think that I could keep that up for 26 miles. But at least I have run all the alcohol out of my system and I don't wake up in the morning feeling guilty!

Tuesday, August 25, 6 miles. Came up to London yesterday to work at ITN for the week. Trying to get here, though, with a wife and three kids by 2.30 in the afternoon is about as knackering as any 15-miler I have yet done. Clothes all sweaty and feeling like a sit down, but instead of that I had to begin the tasks of graphicking for the small screen.

Today was different, however. As I didn't have to be at work until lunchtime I thought I would try a different run, around the streets rather than around the common, so I slipped on to the well-worn rubbish-ridden streets of Clapham and Battersea. Along Lavender Hill I pounded and then down towards Battersea Park and the river. The streets were crowded with people but nobody seemed to notice me. In all those cluttered, noisy, smelly streets nobody seems to raise their tired droopy heads as a runner in bright red running shorts and shirt passes them by. Even the cows in the fields in Banwell have more regard for a human being involved in such a strange activity. But then I suppose living in London is an unnatural existence and hardly likely to make the human race more observant and aware of their environment. People just live a different life there.

I sped over Albert Bridge, all newly painted in white and gold, and along the embankment on the north side of the river. I ran with a good stride, beating the cars and trucks as they waited impatiently in their traffic jams, filling up every available space on the tarmac.

Friday, August 28, 6 miles. After a rest day, some of the will to run had returned. It was strange how I seemed to be told when or when not to run by some body mechanism: today I would go fast or today I would not do a thing. It was as if someone in there was looking after me.

I did the same run as Tuesday, through Battersea Park, along the embankment, over Albert Bridge and home again. I think I ran faster than I had done to date and I relished the feeling of fitness and strength on that hot morning. I felt that I could have kept up that speed for much further than I had set myself. And I enjoyed the feeling of being on my own amongst the dirty, miserable streets and didn't feel part of them at all. I was just passing through: you need to be fit to survive them.

It's peculiar that people don't seem to notice the state of where they live. Perhaps if they did, and it was bad, it would destroy them. But running seems to highlight the environment so much. You seem to feel it, sense it in all manner of ways, respect it, despise it, condemn it, analyse it. Could it be because twentieth-century man hardly touches it any more, or becomes involved with it, but simply observes it from the solitude and isolation of a motor car. Even the seasons mean less and less to people as they move about from one artificial climate into another.

It may be that running makes one more aware or intensifies one's outlook on life, or that it just gives you time to work it all out.

Monday, August 31, 6 miles. I had only just heard about the Wedmore 6-Mile Race. It seemed not a bad idea, I thought, would make a good workout, a quick 6 miles running with a horde of others. At least it would get me used to the idea of running with people alongside me instead of cows. This sort of event usually dragged an odd assortment of beings from out of the woodwork.

Some 150 turned up in a field on this hot and sultry bank holiday, and we gathered together, the fit and the unfit, the lame and the loons. It was an easy task to pick out those with ability and those with little else but endeavour. The running kit varied from the best that money could buy to those which would have required money to take away. Shoes, probably the ultimate status symbol for the aspiring runner, gave clear proof of the multitude's aspirations. Many were new and shiny, bearing the trade marks of some of the most highly prized boots available; then there were the old tennis daps with holes in them, tied up with binding cord, for those whose only concern was to arrive at the finishing line before the pubs shut.

Conversation was as varied as the gear. Odd snippets over-heard formed a weird mixture of hopes, boasts and tension. Running jargon, to one so unused to hearing it, formed a strange backdrop to the broad accents of the supporters who were there in large numbers:

'I did a 39 in the 10s last Saturday at Bath.'

'Not bad. The best I could manage over 7 was just under 30.'

'Not that good, really, considering the course.'

'Mind you, I still expect to do a PB in Manchester.'

There were tales of triumph and success at this and that venue; that Bill and Harry were expecting to reach their peak in time for Windsor and stood a good chance of doing a sub-2.30.

None of these comments did much for my stomach. If I felt like this for the 'Wedmore 6', in aid of the village hall roof fund, what the hell was I going to feel like in New York? Coming up against people who know what they are doing is disconcerting and alarming. It affects the muscle which connects my stomach to my legs and its effect is to paralyse the latter the moment any degree of adrenalin enters the gut. Medical science hasn't found that particular muscle yet, but it will one day. Maybe when they carry out an autopsy on me they will find I am the only person to have such a muscle. Bloody unlucky, that. Perhaps they'll name it after me: 'the Burn Condition'. I'll be in Webster's *Anatomical*.

Certainly, if the others had suffered from the same complaint, after the starting pistol had been fired the several hundred spectators would have witnessed 150 runners standing still: the first Wedmore 6-mile Standing Still Race in aid of the village hall roof fund. But everyone else moved forward at such a ridiculous pace that had I not got out of the way I would have been trampled under several thousand pounds' worth of New Balance, Reebok, Adidas and Brooks. So, with dry lips and now a confirmed carrier of Burn's Condition, I moved forward. By the time I reached the ½-mile marker I found myself in third position, running as if my bum was on fire; by the 1-mile marker I was about twentieth, however, having taken a turn for the worse on the slow incline.

I don't really remember much about the first 2 miles. Fear and tension affected every part of my anatomy. Any ability I possessed at judging time and space had gone completely. I was convinced that I had covered at least 23 miles and that I had been running for some 2 hours, covering each mile in well under 4 minutes, when I approached the first mile marker. 'Silly sods have got it wrong,' I thought. By the 2-mile marker I was positive that the whole race was some sort of farce, some old Somerset ritual where the village invites people from other villages and sends them on a 50-mile run into the bogs and ditches of this legendary county.

After the incline I settled a little. I began to breathe as though I had lungs instead of colanders. Apart from a couple of others who passed me, including a young lad of about twelve who cruised by with such ease and confidence that I felt almost angry, I maintained the position to which I had slipped till the end.

The last mile was evil, though, as they had arranged for that to be a 1 in 6 hill, up towards the finishing line, and what a pig of a hill it was. It would have been easier but there was the sound of footsteps catching me up and the last $\frac{1}{4}$ mile was a positive sprint. All to no avail, however, as I lost the race for twentieth place and felt so ill at the end that I thought I was going to throw up, pass out and cross the finishing line all at the same time, which would have added a little light entertainment for the waiting crowd. But I did recover quickly and recorded a time of 39 minutes, which for a man of my age and lack of finesse in such matters I thought to be good.

I reached home to find out that the sports magazine for which I was writing had just folded and that they would have little use for an article on the New York Marathon. So now what? I was relying on its support a great deal and as the magazine was supposed to be arranging the trip through Seaforth Travel, there was a horrible nagging fear that the whole thing was doomed. And there was still no firm news from the BBC about the film. I wished heartily that I could tie all these ends up. The training was hard enough without all these other complications.

Tuesday, September 1, 3 miles. I managed a gentle meander around the hill but the efforts of the previous day had left me a trifle nonplussed. I was so unconcerned about the run that I didn't even time myself. The ritual had become such a part of my everyday life that I was quite bemused at my sudden lack of interest in it.

I was acutely aware that 'the best laid plans of mice and men' can so quickly go down the shoot. It was similar to what I had experienced not knowing whether I was going to be accepted for the London Marathon — then too I had found it difficult to push hard in training with such doubts. Now it all seemed to be happening again. I felt that I had little control over the proceedings. All I could do was talk to people on the telephone and fill in forms and post them and then what happened after that was up to someone else and they probably didn't care that much about me or running or New York. I felt more than a little impotent as I trundled around the hill. It all suddenly seemed so hopeless that now I can't remember much about what went on apart from the doubts and fears.

When I got home I called the magazine. I received an assurance that the deposits had been paid and was given details of the flight which had been arranged for 20 October. But, yes, there were problems with the magazine...

Why can't things go smoothly? Why do there have to be so many problems all the time? I really could do without all this.

Then Nick phoned to say that the BBC wanted to start filming on 5 October. They were going to make it; it was all arranged.

Wednesday, September 2, 6 miles. I still had the doubts of yesterday as I set off down Riverside, and to add to my troubles my ankle was more painful than I could ever remember it being. I began to run well, however. Then the old feeling of complete exhaustion came over me after about 2 miles and by the time I had reached 3 I was a 'goner'.

I kept thinking of reasons to stop. I still might not even be going to New York. 'You're overdoing it, my old son. Pack it in now. But I can't just stop and walk back now, can I? Oh yes you bloody well can, mate. Yes, well, I know that I can but that's really copping out. Don't bloody care.' The eternal battle between good and evil, fought out on the side of the A317 in the evening twilight.

I struggled the 3 miles home but I felt so tired and weak. I wasn't sure if this was the beginning of a cold or if I was just trying to do too much, or if it was the doubt of going at all that had knocked the stuffing out of me. I yearned for a couple of pints of Guinness, and I resolved to leave off training for a couple of days to see how I would feel.

Chapter Nine

Fantasy and reality. Sound advice from the physiotherapist. Catch 22.

Sunday, September 6, 10 miles. Four days later I had little inclination to run anywhere ever again. My cold had neither the tenacity to turn into something I could get a good blow at or the decency to disappear. It just hung around, making me feel miserable. I had spent the last four days grumping and moping, vegetating and contemplating — so lethargic, so tired; there seemed to be no incentive to push at all.

As Sunday began, however, I bucked up a little. The day was clear and fine. My foot, as long as I didn't walk on it, was fine. My chest, apart from the congestion, was fine. So, with these elements in my favour, I set off. I suppose it was some sort of test to see what the status quo was. Had I blown it completely or had the four days of peace and contentment healed my weary body?

Amazingly, it took me an hour to get myself ready, one hour of pratting about to put on six or seven items of clothing. Then I spent a further ten minutes getting out of the house. What a state I was in. For God's sake pull yourself together, Robert.

As I ran up the High Street I was conscious of how vulnerable I felt — neither cheerful nor healthy. So I took it slowly up to the end, and as I reached the farm, after 1 mile, I began to notice a quickening of pace and some sort of rhythm. I then decided to go to Crooks Peak and along the top of the ridge, along Wavering Down, all 11 miles of it, and having set out my route and stated my objectives I began to feel a little brighter. I waited for the weakness and tiredness to return but it didn't: 3 miles and all was well. I reached Barton and actually began to enjoy it. One or two bad runs could leave me in so much doubt about the sense of doing all this training and of marathon running in general. Is it really a good thing to do for a man of my age and lack of previous experience? But as my confidence returned all these doubts and fears passed away quickly and completely, like a bad dream when you awake in the morning.

Once through Barton I took the bridlepath off to the left and up the steep ascent to the top, past Barton Rocks. Running, walking and then, as the incline proved too much for me, stumbling on all fours over the stony path. But now even the grovelling seemed like fun: playing at mountain goats and keeping a lookout for rabbits and startled skylarks.

I stopped for a while at the top, King of the Castle. I was alone, and far below, in the ultra-violet haze, the Dinky toys dashed along the motorway. I turned and began running down the backbone of Wavering Down, conscious of the breath-taking scenery on both sides. On to the second high point I sped and then down through the woods at the bottom, leaping over the exposed roots of ash trees. I came out at Shute Shelf, just before the busy Bristol-Taunton thoroughfare and then felt the firmness of the road again — no more rocks to avoid or tree roots to fall over, and the totally different sounds of running on tarmac between high stone walls.

I was back home in 1¾ hours: lovely run; new man.

Tuesday, September 8, 4 miles. After the usual indecision I ran right up Hill Path and through the open fields, over the gate and into the wood without stopping. It felt quite easy when taken at a steady plod. Thoughts of New York and BBC films and writing books filled my brain. Whatever had happened to the trees? I could have sworn that I was running through Banwell Woods but the fantasy took over and poor little reality didn't have a chance. And so pleased and fascinated was I with my illusion that as soon as I reached home I went round for a second time to see if I could retrace it. Who needs aeroplane tickets when you can travel like that?

Later Mark called to say that he had had some good luck from Reebok in London who had agreed to sponsor me with running gear. Good old Mark. I was to visit them the following week and collect it. God, wouldn't I look the smarty one!

Wednesday, September 9. I telephoned my friendly physio-therapist, Les Bardsley, in Bristol.

'Hello, Les, it's Rob Burn. I ran in the London Marathon last

March and you treated me for bad legs. Do you remember?'

'Yes, son,' came back the answer in a thick, blunt Blackpool accent.

'Well, I'm running in New York in about a month in the New York City Marathon.'

Pause.

'You don't need a physiotherapist, mate, you need a bloody psychiatrist,' was the well-considered retort.

'Besides that, can I come and see you again, 'cos I can't move my right ankle when I run.'

'Well stop running, you daft sod!'

I think he was trying to save me a small fortune but I did eventually pay him a visit (and the small fortune) and had the inevitable cortisone injection to try to reduce the swelling.

'Now remember, don't run for a while.'

'That's all very well but how do I train for a marathon if I don't run?'

'Listen, lad, if you don't leave off for a few days you'll not even be running for a bus, let alone for a plane to New York.'

Reluctantly I took his advice and called it a day until most of the swelling had gone and I had got thoroughly tired of the hot-and-cold-water treatment which I had to suffer three times daily.

Saturday, September 12, 7 miles. I don't know the name of the enzyme that collects in the body after several days of inactivity, producing withdrawal symptoms, but I know that it does exist. After four days of enforced idleness, the second such period in a fortnight, I was feeling like a frustrated hare. All I wanted to do was to go out for a run — a light canter, a brisk walk, even, anything just to feel the earth flashing by beneath my feet. Talk about being hooked. Heroin has nothing on this. I think they ought to set up centres around the country for running addicts who have to stop through injury, ill health or old age. I could imagine the very place, with high walls and guards in white tracksuits who have to keep rushing out to pick up the weak-willed ones who have succumbed and gone over the top.

By Saturday I just had to do something. Rightly or wrongly I sneaked on my outfit and crept out of the house, convinced that I'd run straight into the physiotherapist. I ran down Riverside. The river had recently been dredged by a tractor with one of those giant scoops at the end of a great arm and was now all clear and pristine. It had suffered something terrible during a recent boat race to mark some occasion or other and had resembled the Suez Canal in the 1950s.

It felt wonderful to be running again: easy, no effort at all. My foot was still hopeless but the rest of me made up for it. I felt so relaxed. I hoped I would feel like this on the day. That would be fantastic. After a marvellous run of about 7 miles I returned home and felt that I had hardly been anywhere. I think I must do a 20-miler soon, foot or not.

Sunday, September 13, 4 miles. Catch 22. Damn my ankle. After yesterday's brave attempt at reasserting my position as an athlete, this part of my anatomy is determined to screw everything up.

The rest of me is fine. I have no other grumbles whatsoever but I find it impossible to run without using both ankles. After yesterday's effort I had plunged it into alternate buckets of hot and then freezing water until my blood had no idea which way it was meant to be flowing. In fact, after 10 minutes of this oldest of tortures, it was impossible for me to tell which bucket had the hot and which the cold. So shall I run and risk knackering up the ankle for good, or risk losing a good deal of the fitness I have attained by leaving off for another few days? Even one or two days without my daily dose of discomfort leaves me frustrated and irritable.

Perhaps I should try to run on the beach! Nice soft sand. No horrid roads. Yes, that's the answer: some fast running along Sand Bay and a quick belt along the top of Woodspring Point. So, with the dog at my side (some hopes), I left the van by Kewstoke Rocks and headed into the strong north wind that blew the Sunday hats off the heads of two middle-aged ladies who were walking arm in arm and exposed their flowery dresses and white petticoats under their matching light blue plastic macs.

Hard along the firm wet sand I pounded, leaving studded patterns as reminders of my route. Further along, where the sand begins to give way to the sea grasses and marshes and the thick sticky mud, great black clouds appeared over the approaching headland and the wind laid the grass level, giving a forecast of what was to come. The dog chased the multitude of wind-propelled plastic bags and half-decaying washing-up-liquid bottles into and out of the sand dunes, appearing at regular intervals along my route to reassure himself that I was still around and thus guaranteeing himself a lift home.

At the foot of the headland, the rocks shielded the weather and gave a false impression of the climate. Feeling strong and healthy, I began the scrambling run up the newly cut path which runs diagonally towards the top. Above, the great black giants continued their games across the sky, but in a weird silence — until, that is, I reached the ridge which opens up the view to the north, an empty expanse across the Bristol Channel. On this side the heavens were black as night and the wind had nothing to push against except me and it did that with such force that it was impossible to run forward. And the rain, which could be seen moving inland in great waves, obliterating the Brecon Beacons and the coastlines of both England and Wales, reached the summit of this small, unprotected headland at about the same time as myself. Suddenly I was drenched. Dog, sussing out the situation quicker than me, turned as if he had seen a great mastiff approaching and scuttled back down the path up which he had just run and into the shelter of the south-facing rocks.

I gave one last look at the dreadful sight ahead and followed him down the slippery track at a speed which was absurd. Once again on the now empty beach, dog and I began to cover the 2 miles back to the van at the far end of the beach at a pace which kept us ahead of the swirling, rushing cyclone. I was convinced that if it actually caught us we would be lifted up and deposited somewhere on the east coast of England. Attempting to avoid such unpleasant weather is quite an incentive to improve one's time over 2 miles. Never had I pushed myself so much over such a distance before, and although both dog and I were overtaken by the storm within ½ mile of the safety of my van, we did manage not to suffer its full impact.

As I slammed the door of the VW camper behind us, the storm dumped itself fairly and squarely on the roof. It was impossible to see out of the windows. The only comparable experience is going through a car wash, when the plastic swirling cylinders tear off any extending appendages and the fierce jets of water find every little hole in the bodywork and begin to fill up the inside and the possibility of drowning becomes a horrid reality.

So there we sat and waited for a while before attempting the drive home, both of us panting and steaming up the windows until the worst of the storm had passed. At least it took my mind off my ankle and the dog's off the mastiff!

Chapter Ten

A rugby training session. 'Super Hero' takes to the road. I seem to be getting it together. A change in my mental attitude. A long run. Doubts and exhilaration. Paranoia sets in. 'After the Lord Mayor's Show.'

Monday, September 14. Rugby training, my first of the season. Not that I actually intended to play this 'rough' sport just five weeks before going to New York, but the idea that the training might do me some good dragged me over to Clevedon and saw me clad in my old rugby gear, behaving like a schoolboy, throwing the white leather ball along the three-quarter line in a fine game of pretend rugby.

It's amazing just how easy it is to play good open rugby when you don't have some great pulp-faced forward pummelling you into the ground. And then they say, 'Great play. Why didn't you all do that last Saturday?' and I think that it's bloody obvious why we didn't do that last Saturday, because if the three-quarter line had ponced about like that and run that straight, there would be five very dead three-quarters lying somewhere on the playing fields of England.

But enough of the niceties. As the heavy rain began to fall again, so the 20 or 30 masochists began playing at war with the assortment of large plastic sacks filled with rocks and broken glass, pushing large contraptions called 'scrummaging machines' from one side of the world to the other and quite hopelessly attempting to pull ourselves up a ladder by using nothing but our little fingers. Such activities are loosely called 'circuit training' and occupy a high percentage of any rugby player's training schedule.

I did this for two hours and I swear that my rigorous roadwork had helped me not one iota. I gave up in disgust as 15-stone men with beer guts and bad breath began to lap me during one of the 'up-and-down-the-pitch' sessions, and I retired with hurt pride to the bar.

Tuesday, September 15. I had arranged to play squash against

Chris Lynham at Churchill, 3 miles away. After 2 miles I ran out of petrol, so dumped the van where it had stopped and set off across the fields, along a so-called public footpath, carrying my kitbag which contained clothes for me to change into after the match. I must have looked a sight, all attired in squash kit, speeding through the rapidly darkening night along this narrow trail which, to my reckoning, bore little resemblance to a footpath. Through a field of contented, cud-chewing cows I lurched and on to something that appeared to be a ditch.

Immediately I found myself up to my knees in a mixture of stagnant water and slurry. What a way to go, stuck in this vile quagmire. I could be here for days. There would of course be a search — possibly lasting 48 hours — and then I would become a statistic: 'gone missing whilst the balance of his mind was disturbed due to the pressure of the oncoming marathon'.

Such horrifying thoughts, and of what would happen to my children, spurred me on and, amid wild gestures, obscene language and some of the most disgusting noises I had ever heard, I began to fight for my life. My racquet flailed above my head to give balance and murder a few of the six million mosquitoes whose home I had so rudely destroyed and who were intent on eating me in revenge.

Eventually I struggled out and resumed my run to the squash club. But my trials were not over, and before reaching safety I was to half-rupture myself on a broken fence as I attempted to run both through it and over it at the same time and plunge head first into a thorn bush which seemed to leap out at me.

At last my destination was reached. As I stood outside the red-brick building with the light shining out through the large glass doors, I must have looked like something out of a horror movie.

'Chris,' said the receptionist, as I walked in, 'the thing from the deep has arrived for your game.'

Wednesday, September 16. Today was the day when I turned myself into an instant runner. This training is all very well but you know that you've really arrived when you can parade yourself around in some of the finest running gear made and today I went to collect it from my sponsor, Reebok.

I met Mike Bowles of that company at ten o'clock in the morning and he began the task of fitting me out for any one of a thousand contingencies which may arise out of running, filming or writing. Shoes, socks, shorts, shirts, sweatshirts, tracksuits, plastic all-weather suits, and a large kitbag to hold the kit of instant professionalism were all supplied. In four short hours I was transformed from an unknown middle-aged runner with high aspirations to a potential world beater: star of TV and track. Who was there on earth that could match me — catch me ? Not one name came to mind as I swanned out of the factory gates, still wearing a pair of the 'Aztec' running shoes which made me feel that I could have run the 120 miles back to Banwell. I showed off all the way home, on the tube, on the train, and then later that evening in the local pub. Oh what a smarty boy I am. How can I possibly lose in New York ?

Thursday, September 17, 7 miles. Four days since my last run and the idea of sitting around at home with all this running gear and not using it is too much for a 'world class' athlete to bear. I had spent most of last night poncing about in front of the full-length mirror on the landing, slipping into this vest and then into those shorts just to work out the best colour combinations, to see which outfit would cut the snazziest dash in New York.

I had put on my red outfit and had just spent 10 minutes abusing myself on Bloody Nora when the desire to run a few miles overcame my fear about wrecking my ankle. I felt like a kid with a new bike for Christmas. I just had to show it off to anyone who would care to stare as I glided past front doors and open windows.

So off down Riverside I went. Running with 'proper' running shoes for the first time made me realise how absurd it was to have attempted anything without them. There would be no more of the bone grinding and ligament stretching of previous outings. In their place came a sort of floating feeling as heel met road and hardly made a sound. The push-off was so much better too — my toes projected my feet further than before, so that at last I seemed to be gliding over the surface of the road instead of trying to plough my way through it. What a difference!

Feeling more and more like 'Super Hero', I thought I'd try the humorously named Fartlek Training Method. This consists of running quickly for a few hundred yards, then returning to a more normal speed, and repeating the procedure. Although I could feel the pressure on my ankle, it was noticeably easier with the new shoes and I hoped that they would make all the difference over the next few weeks. I continued the quick-slow-quick-slow shuffle for the first 3 miles and then ran the rest of the circuit at a steady trot. As I reached Summer Lane the rain began falling. It was the first time that I could remember running on roads in such a heavy rain. Before I had travelled much further the road surface had turned into a ford. My virgin vest and shorts were wet through and my shoes were throwing up spray like tyres in a telly ad.

It was beginning to grow dark prematurely as the clouds covered up the last remaining patches of early evening sky. Lights from passing cars cast multi-coloured reflections in the wet, black tarmac as remote, isolated and dry, drivers sped past the most sartorial of drowned rats. The noise from my shoes had changed to a regular squelch as they filled up with water then came down on the liquid mirror, squeezing themselves empty.

It took me 50 minutes to cover the 7 miles and I smiled with contentment as I soaked in the bath. I seemed to be getting it together.

Saturday, September 19, 3 miles. Up early. I must run every day, get back into the habit of waking up with a run. Now there's a motto. I must do something each morning even if it's just the 3 miles round the hill. Then I can let the rest of the day take care of itself.

I did 5 minutes of exercising, the usual standing in front of the half-open bedroom window in a pair of Y-fronts, looking like some margarine commercial. Then followed 10 minutes' wrestling with Bloody Nora. One thing to be said for doing all this preparation is that by the time I do eventually get round to running, I feel as if all the hard work is over.

I set off up the High Street with my arms dragging on the ground beside me, checking to make sure that I wasn't pulling the damned rowing machine behind. I felt fit, I couldn't deny it, and so resolved to run as quickly as I could. I got into some sort of rhythm quickly and again found the new shoes to my liking. Heel down first, push off with my toes, running, moving, speeding over the hard, smooth road.

I amazed myself by actually running quickly up Wynt Hill. I had never done that before. What pleasure. What success. Deep breathing all the way up. Although I arrived at the top gasping I didn't lose pace and recovered rapidly.

I managed the run in 21 minutes which was the fastest yet and a clear indication that things were getting better. I had a feeling of great satisfaction, of proof that I was achieving something.

After a quick bath I went on to play a squash match: five sets and I still had some energy left at the end. Who is this man?

Sunday, September 20, 20·3 miles. I must have been dreaming about long-distance running. The first thing I thought of as I woke was that today was going to be the day for a good thrash. Things had gone well last week and the shoes had seemingly made a world of difference to my ankle.

I dressed in my running kit, made a cup of tea and sat in the kitchen. For the first time that I could remember, I actually planned out where I was going to run: Riverside, Worle, Kewstoke, Old Pier, along the sands at Weston, Uphill, Hutton and Banwell. There's been such a change in my mental attitude. I might even end up paying bills on time or getting my car through its MOT before it runs out.

Beginning a long run is very different from attempting something like a 5- or 6-mile one. For the first mile or so there is a sense of coming to terms with the distance ahead, of trying to decide what sort of speed is likely to be suitable. The idea is, I suppose, to get into a rhythm which will take you all the way round without too much deviation in speed. Today it was noticeable that I seemed to settle on a speed which was faster than I had tried before, more ambitious. If I was going to try to do the marathon in under 3.30, this was the sort of pace at which I would need to run.

After 8 or 9 miles I had reached the Old Pier and took a quick sneaky glance at a clock through the window of the hotel there to see how long it had taken. I seemed to need some sort of proof that I was running well, that I had done the distance in good time — a sort of visual pat on the back.

At the 10-mile point, the large clock on the front of the bus station certified that I had so far been running for 1 hour 10 minutes. I then ran along the promenade rather than risk the waterlogged sand, which is capable of pulling your calf muscles to bits. The crowds had thinned out a little as I reached the end of the promenade and ran on to the firmer, drier sands of Uphill.

I was running well. To be able to reach this point and still feel fit was a real boost. I remembered doing this run before the London Marathon and how tired I had felt. Comparatively I was now feeling far stronger and keen to go further. I changed my route, along the Bridgwater Road to Bleadon, and returned through Loxton and Christon, thus making a 17-mile run into a 20-plus one. The flat roads gave me no problems but the steep incline out of Bleadon was hard. Two girls on a swing told me to 'keep my knees up' and chanted, 'One, two, one, two' as I passed them: sound advice. I gained height, out of the village, and soon the houses and chanting girls were out of sight and my reward for the steep push upwards was the downward trip on the other side. I was still maintaining a good pace after 14 miles, along the quiet lane: no shuffling, still pushing. Thank God for my new booties.

Into Loxton I sped and along the slow painful road which leads out of it. It is steep even in a car. On foot, after 15 miles of running, it was horrific. Time to turn my head off, I thought, and let my body get on with it. The hill lasts for about ¾ mile and at the top my legs had gone. It was a terrible strain to keep going. I began to feel faint, past it. At one point I thought I was going to black out and had thoughts of being picked up by a passing motorist and getting carted off to the Weston General. I thought of the so-called 'wall' which one hears so much about — when you just run out of energy and that's the end of it. Perhaps it's not within my capability to run that fast for that long ...

I did manage to keep running after I'd climbed out of the village, although the strange feeling of not actually being conscious didn't leave me completely. The thought that I had reached the 'wall' faded a little and I decided that it was simply the effects of the terrific effort of the hill. By Christon I had recovered, thankfully, and reality was returning in small doses. The run down the hill from Christon to the south side of Banwell Hill was painful in different places from the uphill effort of 10 minutes before. Trying to hold yourself back is difficult and after some 18 miles takes a bit of doing. As I ran over the motorway bridge, my shadow was well and truly 'squashed' by a passing truck, which summed up the way I felt.

Coming in towards the foot of the hill, I began thinking of the film but my mind was unable to focus sensibly. I suppose such a time was not the best to try objectively to plan out a film script of an event about which I knew nothing and which had no ending. What would it be? Comedy? Tragedy? Unfinished? Nothing at all if training went wrong — all these recurring nightmares of pulled muscles and twisted ankles.

The field of cows to my left took on the appearance of a crowd of ladies in black and white bikinis lying on a beach, soaking up the sun. God, I was going insane.

And what about the film's title? Endless combinations filled my head: 'In the long run', 'Mind over patter', 'One man and his jog'. Hey, that's not bad, and I laughed to myself as I began the last of the slow inclines which led round Banwell Hill and eventually to the High Street.

I experienced an amazing feeling of exhilaration when I finally reached home. I had done my long run. I had done it well and felt healthy as I walked into the kitchen.

'How far, Dad?' asked Lucy.

'About 20,' I said, making no attempt to hide my pride.

84

'Cor, Dad, that's good and you don't even look tired,' she said, and I began to feel unbearably smug. I didn't ache much and felt that I could have gone further.

That afternoon I drove round the same circuit just to see how far it was. 20·3 miles. Great! It really did seem a hell of a long way. Still, old son, remember, 'After the Lord Mayor's Show' and all that. Be prepared for a few bad ones as well before New York and don't get too disgruntled.

Wednesday, September 23, 8 miles. I left off running for a couple of days after the epic of Sunday, although I did manage rugby training and a game of squash just to keep an edge. Today, however, I had decided to get the old early-morning call going again. I'd set the alarm clock for 7.30, determined to prove to the damned thing once and for all that it held no fear for me. From now on it was new putty in my hands.

At 7.30 I threw the clock out of the window and into the garden. I felt as if I was getting the cold that had hit the rest of the family over the last few days and which had given me thoughts of living in a hotel for the next fortnight and having all my food brought to me on a tray. Then it could be left outside the door and when the bearer had retreated I could collect it. That way I would not have to see anybody and I wouldn't go down with something nasty at the last moment. I was quite paranoid: 'Everybody's out to get me with their nasty little bugs.'

At 9.00 I finally arose and, feeling marginally more awake and slightly less irritable, managed a gentle run around the hill. It was not strenuous, but it cleared my head a little.

Now, where did that alarm clock go?

Thursday, September 24, 6 miles. I still didn't feel up to much, but the nagging deep inside me made me attempt the 6 miles to Locking village and back. Almost before I'd reached the main road a couple of hundred yards away, I knew I was wasting my time. Should I stop or carry on? Should I push harder? I really didn't know which was the right thing to do.

I carried on, but I could see another rest period coming up. Was I going down with something? Or was it just the after effects of the 20-miler at the weekend? Talk about 'after the Lord Mayor's Show' indeed. I had half-prepared myself for a bad run but this was terrible. A long run obviously took me much longer to get over than I had realised. By the time I'd reached Locking my strides had shrunk to a shuffle. How I managed to keep going I don't know, but it must have taken me an hour to get round. Tomorrow I would do no running or violent exercise.

When I reached home I cancelled my squash court and decided that I'd go swimming instead.

Chapter Eleven

Running in a water bed. I break the habit of a lifetime and don't go to the Lion. I seem to have run through the seasons. I consider a run of some 3,514 miles.

Saturday, September 26, 7 miles. I think winter is beginning to arrive. It's cool today. I spent most of the day sawing and splitting the great chunks of pine which had been well stacked in my garden for the winter months. The best thing about wood fires is that they make you warm twice: once when you cut the wood and once when you burn it.

At 6.30 I began to run a tub to wash away the layer of wood chippings which covered my body when suddenly guilt struck and I climbed into my running gear instead of my bath. As it was getting late and cool, and because I had been taking exercise, I wore my tracksuit with the plastic rainsuit on top of that. I ran up the High Street and thought that I'd do the usual Riverside run in reverse. It was a distance of about 7 miles.

The effect of running while wearing so much and with the plastic suit on top is two-fold. Not only can the rain not get through to you, but whatever is inside cannot get out either. So within a mile or two the temperature inside the suit goes up a couple of hundred degrees and anything worn underneath becomes sodden — it's like running inside a water bed.

Even with the added weight of the imprisoned moisture, however, I was pleased with my efforts. I ran well and felt that I could increase my speed at times as I dashed along the wet, muddy roads that wind themselves in and out of the undulating countryside. If only I could feel like this in a month's time . . .

The run took me 50 minutes and I lost over 3lb in weight. I filled the bath again and bathed the bath of the righteous.

Saturday, September 27, 3 miles. On television I had witnessed the training methods used by Alan Wells. During his training runs he had been doing various weird exercises, legs kicking high in the air, huge overdone strides apparently in imitation of Steve Austin, and heavy breathing — taking great lungfuls of fresh air, inhaled right down to the legs.

Whatever is good enough for Alan Wells is good enough for me. So off I went around the hill for a 3-mile jaunt. I must have looked stupid, all tarted up in my blue and yellow boots with matching blue vest and shorts, prancing along an English country lane. Arms and legs flew akimbo along with much grunting and puffing: a demented daddy-long-legs. I think I was more conscious of my appearance than of what I was meant to be doing and so kept a cautious lookout for fellow travellers. When they did appear I quickly broke into a trot and ran normally until they had passed out of sight. Such antics are so unbecoming. 'If you are going to make a fool of yourself, Rob, I think you should at least do it in private.'

Monday, September 28, 3 miles. I began my winter session as an art college lecturer. Being an 'associate' means that I have been able to do all that is required of me between the months of September and April, so leaving a good period of time for me to work on my own, at home in my studio. Today, however, I was back in the taste emporium and at lunchtime broke the habit of a lifetime by not going to the pub. Instead I changed into my tracksuit and smarty boots and, having checked that no one was looking, sneaked along the corridors of culture and out into Ashton Park.

It was eight months since I last ran around the park, situated on what was the Somerset side of the Avon Gorge, a great hole in the landscape that has held back the waters of the River Avon for thousands of years and the building speculators of Bristol for the last fifty. The park at one time belonged to the Smyth family and their recently renovated mansion is still to be seen in the centre. It is a fine, well-landscaped, hilly estate, bordered by high stone walls, three lodge gates and several well-cultivated woods. To circumnavigate the area one must cover a distance of some 6 or 7 miles. Today it brought back memories of training for the London Marathon, rather as Clapham Common had done earlier in the year — memories of days and energy long gone.

I decided to go up to the suspension bridge, through the park and back down to the art college. This would be a strenuous run of some 3 miles as the climb up to the bridge is a hard one and lasts for about 1 mile and today, with the sun shining on the houses which lie upon the hills in Clifton, it quickly brought back the sweat as well as the memories.

I timed myself. I could remember doing the same run in the summer in about 23 minutes and wondered how I would compare today. The steepness of the hill came as a shock as time makes one forget the pain incurred on such a run in days long past. At the top and once into the park, I managed to begin breathing again, and the run down, past the deer enclosure and three 'proper-looking' runners coming towards me, was fast and enjoyable. There was the usual 'hello-hello' and then back to the college.

It had taken me 19 minutes. Well, well, well!

Wednesday, September 30, 6 miles. One is sufficient, two is too many and three's not enough. When I first heard that, it was applied to the art of beer drinking, but it's equally applicable to running. An insatiable thirst ... want more ... so the just running 3 miles of late has become about the same as going all the way to a pub for a half-pint. Once you're there, you might as well do the job properly. God! Think of a pint!

At lunchtime I did the run up to the suspension bridge again, along Bridge Road and into Ashton Park. This time I extended my run by some 3 miles by making a circuit of the golf course which lies at the very top of the park. After the hardness of the terrible slog up the hill, the course was wonderfully flat and soft underfoot.

On the way back, and once through Twenty-Acre Wood, panoramic views of Bristol opened before me. The atmosphere was hazy and a dull, brownish shadow hung over the multitude of houses and factories. Back into college I sped, feeling fit and well, for a quick show off in the bar and a glass of orange juice.

Thursday, October 1, 14 miles. October: twenty-five days to go and my stomach gave a quick impression of a cement mixer at the thought of it.

I got home about 5.30 and decided to have another attempt at a fairly long run. I must have been motivated by some sort of suicidal tendency, I think, as I knew what would happen. But I did think it was important to face up to the different set of problems which were the consequence of anything over 10 miles — the tiredness, which of late seemed to last for several days afterwards, the stress on the muscles and ligaments and of course the aggravation from my ankle, although in fairness it had been easier with the new shoes and improved skill in running techniques.

I seemed to have run through the seasons. It was about 6.30, nearly dark and rather cold. I decided to go through the village and along the Locking road towards Weston. I would run to the Old Pier and back through Weston. In a way it was rather like choosing food, naturally selecting what you need most: a strange diet of miles and company, or woods and solitude. Today I would have a small portion of people, a large helping of traffic and houses, followed by rocks and cool sea breezes. Two silly giggling women walking along the Locking road gave me the impression that people were 'off' today, but I stuck with the rest of the original menu.

Compared to the terrible run to Locking last week, I felt good. I was running well. I had three layers of clothing on — shorts and vest, tracksuit and waterproofs — to keep out the approaching winter. I was nice and snug as I ran past the air force camp and on into Weston — a glowing bundle.

Weston came quickly. The 5 miles passed easily and the endless rows of twenties semi-detached boarding-houses which line the main road into the town showed forlornly that most of the visitors had gone home long ago. Sad little white plastic 'Vacancies' signs hung down from in front of the nylon-netted bay windows.

But the landscape passed quickly. I seemed to be in New York more than Weston-super-Mare, and soon the boarding houses were replaced by skyscrapers, negroes replaced land-ladies, and the fish and chip shops, which are innumerable here, were exchanged for MacDonald's hamburger restaurants.

As I turned to start the return trip, the winds were blowing harder, though this time behind me, helping rather than hindering. Should I run to Worle, where Pat was waiting to collect Lucy from her gymnastics class, or should I go all the way home?

How familiar this discussion was. How easily I was able to wrap it up in a neat bundle of pretence. The cunning arguments I could use to support my weaker self were endless: that it was too dark to run on the roads or too cold and wet; that it was about the same distance really if you took account of the bends, when I knew perfectly well that it was at least 4 miles shorter; that I'd like to watch Lucy do a few of her back flips as I hadn't seen her do them for a while . . .

Run, Robert, run . . . all the way home. That's what you're here for. And I was quite cross with myself for allowing such cowardly thoughts into my head.

So I did run. I covered 14 miles in about 1 hour 45 minutes if you don't count the excursion to New York. It was 3514 if you do. Apart from my ankle, which was giving several nasty short sharp stabs of pain towards the end, I arrived home well pleased with my efforts and my latest triumph over temptation.

Sunday, October 4, 16 miles. A damp, miserable Sunday morning. My son Tom was off to rugby practice, bless him, only six and loving the game. Mind you, if he should ever get hold of the ball in one of these matches he might go off it with a rush.

As I began my warming-up exercises, I decided that I fancied a long run as I hadn't been out for a few days and Sundays now seemed synonymous with hills and lonely byroads. Just in case my foot did get bad I had taken to hiding 5p about my person to make that emergency phone call.

Off I sped in the wet morning, this time without my waterproofs as on any run over 10 miles I thought I'd burst into flames. I felt fairly certain that I'd now sorted out my correct pace and rhythm. If I could stick with that all the way around New York I should be able to do it in about 3¾ hours. I had my watch on, which really was daft as all I did was keep looking at it. I don't normally wear one, in 'real life' or in running, but the last few outings and the need to find out if I was working well had driven me to strapping on the old chronometer before I set off.

I was running steadily, heels first on the road every time. The rain was keeping off. Along the Weston Road I went, over the motorway intersection, through Worle and up the steep hill towards Kewstoke. Painful, always painful — I could feel the ankle and the effects of Thursday's run, but couldn't decide which was worse.

I reached Sand Bay and ran along the sea wall. It had taken me 1 hour to do the outward journey, and I turned to go home, passing the hosts of indigenous assorted coloured caravans which daub the sea front. The return trip was as good as the outward one had been. I did feel weary but managed to keep a good bounce in my feet. Thoughts of New York now seemed to be constantly in my head, blocking out the natural landscape and sounds. There was not enough room in my head for much more. I had even dreamt of New York last night. How the whole think had taken over my life, my thoughts, my mind! What would happen after it was all over? What would I do with myself? Time on my hands. Still, Robert, let's get the race over with first and let the rest of life take care of itself.

My journey home took 1 hour, and I was delighted to have proved to myself that I could run for 2 hours at the same speed.

Chapter Twelve

Filming commences.

Tuesday, October 6. Today we began filming at 6.30 in the morning. The reality of all those abstract conversations and theories had begun.

I had been awake many times during the night, worrying, thinking, going through this and that shot. At about 5.50 I got up and dressed, giving up for good the appalling mixture of emotions and locations which had made up my nightmarish slumber. It was black outside and could have been any time. I made tea in the kitchen to wash away the tiredness and sat for a while, trying to make my head a little clearer. Then I left the house and wandered down the quiet street towards the square to see if the crew had arrived. They were to 'RV' there at 6.30 to get some 'sleepy' shots of the village as dawn broke.

The square was empty. I was seized with a fear that the whole thing was a joke and there wouldn't be a film. I made a second sortie after returning home to refortify myself with more tea and this time was rewarded by the sight of a big grey Volvo lying purring opposite the Bell. They were here. It had begun.

The plan was that we would do some running shots around Banwell, general views from the church tower and a running sequence down Riverside, and then move on round to Weston and see how we got on from there. To this end I had arranged with the vicar to have the church opened at 6.30; that Arthur the farmer should ride his bike down the High Street; and that Alan the milkman should be delivering the daily pint — all to give an air of 'early morning' to the proceedings. Thus I found myself taking on the role of star, coordinator, prompter, cook, location supervisor, transport organiser, fashion consultant, technical advisor and sound effects man.

I therefore considered my role in this film to be fairly important and as the crew went off to get some early-morning shots of Riverside and Banwell awakening, I ran up the High Street to try to drag Arthur out of his bed. At least he was up and appeared dressed to kill in his cowmuck-ridden bags, his old green anorak and his red bobble hat, complete with straw. His pre-war bicycle with its 2-pint milk churn slung over the handlebars made up the picture.

Now for Alan the milk, who was nowhere to be seen. By the time the crew came back from Riverside, complete with film of suspicious locals peering through their net curtains, I had located him in Arthur's kitchen, having a cup of tea.

So at last we were ready to begin: 'Action!' I ran out of the side gate as Alan was performing his allotted task of depositing three bottles of farm fresh milk into a battered plastic milk bottle holder at the side of the house.

'' 'Ello, Rob,' he said, in a fine steady voice.

'Hi, Alan,' I replied in well-rehearsed surprise.

'Goin' to win, then?' he said.

'You're joking,' said I.

'Cut,' said the voice that had declared action earlier on. 'Fine, marvellous, now if we can just do that again, but this time if you would look at each other when you are speaking, otherwise marvellous, wonderful, super.'

Back into the garden we trooped.

'Action.'

Out through the gate.

'' 'Ello, Rob.'

'Hi, Alan,' I said with a long loving gaze into the eyes of the milkman.

'Goin' to win, then?'

'You're joking,' and a little run off down the road.

'Cut. Fine, wonderful, okay. Once more and then I think that should be about okay. A bit slower I think, otherwise super.'

During all this activity Arthur looked on in disbelief from the security of his own back gate: six grown men playing at making films. Whenever I looked at him he was either trying not to laugh, laughing or trying to stop laughing. All this gear — cameras, clapper boards, boom mikes — toys for grown-ups.

Then we progressed to the church. We were about to enter the door which leads up into the tower when:

'Yew can't go up there wi'out I,' growled the voice of the churchwarden from out of the shadows of the vestry. 'They baint safe, they bells. Might be upright an' that be dangruss, see.'

'Pardon?' I said.

'They bells — might be upright.'

'Oh, I see,' I said, though I didn't for the life of me. 'I'm not going to swing on them, you know. In fact we're not going into the bell tower part at all — just on to the roof.'

'Oh, I see,' said the warden and, after a second reassurance that none of us would play at Quasimodo, he led the crew up the 132 steps to the top of the tower.

Arthur and I waited below for the little group to appear over the fifteenth-century stonework and watched as they poked their various items of equipment out between the fast-failing masonry and the faces of the gargoyles. When all was ready, off we went down Church Street, Arthur on his bike with me running beside him.

'Fine,' shouted the gargoyle, 'but could we do it once more, the churchwarden has just fallen over.'

'Christ!' I thought. 'That's a bit tragic.'

'Over what?' I shouted.

'Over on to his bum. On the slippery roof. He's OK but he knocked the camera.'

'God help us,' I thought. 'I'll never get through this. It's only 8.30 and we've already had one missing milkman, one farmer gone insane and a churchwarden committing suicide by leaping to his death.'

'Off we go again then, Arthur.'

'Right, Robbie,' said the rustic riding man. Then, 'How far do we go?'

'Don't know,' said I.

'Yer, maybe they gone an' fergott'n uz.'

So we stopped at Bow Bridge and wandered back to the church.

'Everything OK?' I enquired.

'Fine,' said the producer, 'marvellous, couldn't have gone better.'

'We didn't hear you say stop,' I said, panting a little from the ¾-mile excursion.

'Oh, sorry, forgot about that,' he said.

'Doesn't matter,' I replied and Arthur, taking the price of a few pints for his part, rode off into the countryside chuckling to himself in the knowledge that he would get more sense out of his cows.

At 9.30 we moved away from the church and the picturesque shots of Banwell and returned to the house. This time it was the turn of the chickens: the rural cliché bit. Clive the camera, Richard the clapper and Tom the boom all pranced around in the straw inside the chicken house as the birds looked on in bewilderment.

This was followed by a quick shot of the kids walking up the garden looking as if they'd stepped out of *Cider with Rosie* and then we went inside the kitchen for breakfast. Before we all ate, however, there had to be shots of Pat cooking, me freshly laundered and looking neat and tidy, and the kids eating healthy breakfasts.

'Just act normally,' said Paul the producer. 'Forget we're here.'

Some hopes, though Tom did come out with a classic 'I don't want to go to school today' line which I hoped would stay in the film. It looked so rehearsed and wasn't. There then followed the ceremonial eating of the enormous breakfast which had been recorded on film for posterity. The hearty feast went a long way to making up for the silly start to the day.

After we had eaten to the full we moved off down Riverside to get some 'pleasant' shots of the river and reflections of me, as a continuation of the last shot taken from the church tower. Then there took place the tracking shot of me trailing along behind a car with the cameraman hanging out of the window. Now, a few yards of this tracking behind a car may be all very well but I had just eaten an enormous breakfast and drunk at least a gallon of tea since six o'clock, and running behind a Ford Cortina at 15 mph for about a mile is no joke. Surely there should be a stand-in for these parts? I'd have a word with the producer about it.

'Paul.'

'Yes, Rob, that's fine, I think we'll just do another shot from round the corner and that will be perfect.'

'Actually, Paul, what I was going to mention was ...'

'Oh yes, the slow-motion bit. Good, I'd forgotten that. We'll do that after the next sequence.'

And so it went on, the disenchantment, the fatigue. By midday we had reached the motorway, and I felt as if I had run 120 miles. God help me, please — I can't keep this up much longer. And as if my prayers were answered, the rain which had been threatening all morning began to fall in torrents and wiped out any thoughts of further outdoor shots that day.

We therefore returned to Banwell and began shooting in my studio, which we had planned for the following day. I had hoped to spend the evening shovelling out the rubbish and sorting out some of the work which we could put on film, but as it turned out there wasn't time. During the 10 minutes it took the crew to erect the banks of lights and find the most suitable camera angles, I cleared up as best I could.

We eventually finished at seven o'clock. I was absolutely exhausted. I could hardly stand up. The thought of doing anything else that night was inconceivable and Pat and I crashed out down at the Bell for an evening meal. How on earth was I going to survive another six days of this? No wonder all those superstars begin to act in the most peculiar way.

Saturday, October 10, 7 miles. After the madness of the last few days' filming, during which I felt as if I had run round the world and back, had given lectures and held endless seminars on 'the need for design in modern marathon running', had proved irrefutably that it is possible to live without sleep and, if asked suddenly where I was at that point in time, would have been totally unable to say, I rose from my bed at 9.00 for a run. I felt an urgent need to take the air and move continuously for a few miles instead of a few hundred yards.

My tracksuit, the one used for filming, was still drying out after two days, following the unrepentant 'instant sweat' spray with which Nick was obsessed, and I therefore had a welcome change of gear. Although I may have looked different, however, I didn't feel it. As soon as I reached Riverside, back came the old thoughts: the filming, the writing, New York. The running was continuous but so was the absurd mental activity. And although my legs may have got it together, my head had not. It was incapable of sorting out what was happening on the outside. It had obviously suffered some sort of identity crisis and wasn't sure what its present role in life was meant to be. It refused to digest that random selection of thoughts that flowed in and out of the one or two cells that were still functioning. The green fields of Banwell surrounded the Statue of Liberty and on the far side of the two-hundred-year-old bridge that spans the mighty waters of the Banwell river I could already see the 16,000 runners gathering.

It was as though my brain was having an attack of St Vitus' dance. No amount of concerted effort on the part of the rest of me could make the slightest degree of difference. It was a mad, mad world of unreal images and thoughts. Now and again my brain would consider joining up with the rest of me — say, as I was about to roll in front of a passing Land-Rover or fall into one of the many rhines — but that was only a transient effort. Then it would continue with its unilateral declaration of independence and rush off somewhere else. After some 5 miles I accepted my idiot state of mind, giving up any attempt to pull it back into one piece. Just as long as we all ended up back at Number 20 High Street at roughly the same time.

And so it was. The familiar paths and roads, hedges and buildings along the lane to the Weston road and back through Way Wick. I vaguely remember running well, that there were many people on horseback, that the roads were wet, slippery in places from a recently passed herd of cows and what they had left behind, that they were littered with debris strewn by the

98

strong winds of the last few days. The usual Great Danes bid me their usual noisy welcome from behind the high hedges and strengthened gates, and that was fine by me as long as they stayed there. And I wondered if the peripatetic film crew had yet arrived for the third day's filming. Knowing how exhausting the last two had been, I had reservations about the 7-mile run I had just undertaken, especially at the speed at which I had tackled it.

We all arrived at the house together. I made tea and changed from one load of wet running gear into the still-damp grey tracksuit. We refilled the 'instant sweat' bottle, loaded up the VW camper with equipment and crew, and drove up to the plantation high above Christon as the rain, which had been so predictable, began to fall and, from the look of the heavy clouds, gave no encouragement that it would ever stop.

Some hours later I arrived home completely blown away. I was wet, cold, tired, mentally unsound and convinced that I would die quite soon. All I wanted to do was lie down and go to sleep.

'Did it go all right?' enquired Pat from the comfort of the living room, and then, without waiting for the negative reply, 'I've arranged a squash match for you in 45 minutes. Didn't know if you'd want to play or not but it is a box match and you do need to get as many in as you can before New York.'

Oh Lord, how am I going to survive the next couple of weeks?

Chapter Thirteen

I begin to lose control. Mental and physical inertia prevents me from running. My recovery and last long training run to Woodspring Priory on a terrible night. Steak and chips and a pint of Guinness.

Monday, October 12, 7 miles. Lecturing and freelance work were piling up — stacking on top of each other like planes at Heathrow. So many things to do before New York.

I felt tired from the efforts of the weekend and an early start today didn't help, but I had to get certain things sorted out for the lectures. I lashed into the students again as soon as I began — such bad temper and intolerance. They seemed as bored with me as I was with them. Perhaps it was because there was so much going on in my life that I just hadn't the time to think hard enough about them and their work, their moods and objectives. They, on the other hand, seemed to have so much time, or is it that I'm just jealous that they have no responsibilities? My patience, or rather the lack of it, will not allow me really to find out what they need. All I could think of was me.

It was therefore a bad day at work. I was even beginning to feel real resentment about the time I spent at college. So I arrived home in a grumpy mood, only to find that Pat had pulled the pantry to bits in a futile search for the family of mice who had moved in some time during the previous month or two and who had made themselves quite at home with a wholesome diet of Weetabix and Sainsbury's Country Style Stuffing Mix.

'Thank God you're back early, give me a hand with this bloody pantry, will you, I can't stand those mice any longer.'

Now in all fairness to Pat, I could understand her feelings about the mice, and the sight of mouse droppings on top of the tinned tomatoes was offputting and unhygienic to boot, but rebuilding the pantry was the very last thing I felt like doing at that time.

'It wouldn't take you long just to do it, would it?' she said.

'What?' I said.

'Just to fill up the holes and put back the wood.'

'What?' I said. 'Couldn't you have just left it until we got back from the States? I mean, of all the things I've got to do . . . I'm going out for a run!' And I left a seething Pat knee-deep in tins of this and that, enough to last for years should there be a nuclear war whilst we were in the US of A.

Instantly the whole world stopped. There was silence, wonderful peace. All the bottled-up aggravation of the day, all the trivia and pointlessness, just faded away, dissipated over the quiet roads, lanes and fields. Running is magic — 'Abracadabra!' All the lights went down and the sounds were turned off and I ran out of the village and on into the quiet sympathetic night and it was as if I could have run and run and run for ever, without stopping.

Running was making more sense to me now than anything else. There was no fuss, no complications. I needed to get away into a different world and a different way of existing and thinking.

I did the 7 miles down Riverside. It had replaced the run round the hill as a daily task and was now so familiar that there was little to surprise me or hold my attention for long. And if my last trip out had been difficult to handle, this was clearly going to prove impossible.

The miles seemed to be running past me as I stood still. Effortless. The same pace, the same rhythm, past the spots where the 'instant sweat' spray had played havoc with my tracksuit during filming and where the tracking shots had gone on and on, far beyond the planned 200-yard dash, and my legs had nearly dropped off.

By the time I had reached the Brewer's Arms I had drifted hopelessly off into my own little world of fantasy and contentment, free from arguments and mouse droppings, students and assessments. It was like pulling the plug out of the bath, letting all the murky water drain noisily away and then refilling it with whatever you wanted: up to the brim with New York and films and rich fantasies.

I ran fast, all the way round. It took 47 minutes and I felt so high that nothing else seemed to have much meaning other than the running.

Tuesday, October 13, 7 miles. I am sure that the OS map will one day prove categorically that it is longer and harder to run the Riverside run anticlockwise. The fact that my brain was befuddled did not help. In fact, I feared that it might well explode before the day was out, but I would swear that it was ten per cent longer and twenty per cent more difficult to get round in that direction.

After another day of utter turmoil, leaping from one thought to another, I escaped this mortal coil at 6.30 and refused to speak to anyone or to do any work at all (that included the long war against the pantry mice) until after my run. I exercised first in the usual way — this was now a familiar part of my training — and then off I went down the High Street and into the village. I think one of the reasons that I had stopped experimenting with different routes was that I was incapable of making any new decisions. To contemplate new, exciting, untried paths would have taken up too much energy and my head just wasn't capable of handling such daring ideas. Simple thoughts, one at a time, were about right for me at that moment. Anything else, any secondary buzz of excitement, could well have sent me into the loony house forever. So I stuck to what I knew and eliminated any thoughts of discovery and creativity.

My legs were groaning a little on the way round. They felt tired and weary after the continual daily exercise. Long distances on consecutive days really tell. But I did manage to keep the same rhythm going, slowing only to allow passing tractors or cars or swans or snarling teeth-gnashing dogs (I was sure one of those monstrous things would get me soon) to pass.

The day was cold and windy, the coldest by far since I had begun the running in May. I hid inside my thick woolly track-suit. The landmarks seemed inconspicuous and unimportant and the tiredness in my legs of little consequence. Tired or not, they would get me round. And that is where I came in.

I seemed to be running quickly, even faster than yesterday.

But I took about 5 minutes longer to do the 7 miles. This way round there were two long hills to ascend, both evil and despicable. In the other direction — clockwise — there was just the one main incline that seemed to be spread over a distance of about a mile. There is the horrid, quick sod of a slope at the bottom of High Street, but together they did not add up to anything near the horrors of the anticlockwise run. Should I be able to prove this as a fact one day, when I have more time to contemplate such issues, the laws of physics will be shot away completely and Newtonian Theory will be a thing of the past.

Thursday, October 15. The previous two days had passed without a run. Not that I had planned it that way — it just happened that the ever-increasing list of 'things to do' had extended to the length of a seven-year-old boy's Christmas list and most of my working day was spent zooming around the art college. I must have easily run a dozen or so miles in the course of my duties. I spent hours, or so it seemed, writing, shouting, lecturing, reading and copying endless notes on the Xerox machine (oh, that I could make a duplicate of myself so easily, and for 5p at that!). I didn't worry about not having run as I had covered a lot of ground during the previous days. What did cause me anxiety was the number of confusing thoughts that filled my head.

I eventually got home at 7.30 to find the tickets for New York along with the information for the 'fun run' from Westminster to Heathrow on Sunday. This was for all those runners going from England who fancied carrying out their last long training run in front of the TV cameras and in the company of others who were probably in the same sort of condition. The adrenalin began its familiar trip around the inside of my stomach at the same time as Art Garfunkel's 'Heart in New York' came over the radio. Again I tried to put in perspective exactly what it was that I was trying to achieve.

I could not cram any more thoughts into my head. It was full up. I wished I could resort to a bottle of something, just to take the edge off. And tomorrow I had to do a day's lecturing at St Martins School of Art in Covent Garden. That meant leaving home at about 6.30 a.m. I would have to do a run in the morning or perhaps at lunchtime.

Friday, October 16. Today I did nothing at all. I felt absolutely worn out. The day's work was pleasant but uneventful and didn't seem to rate anywhere on my list of priorities. It was just another expenditure of time and energy that I could have well done without.

I seemed to spend most of my time explaining about the marathon and the film and the book and precious little talking about graphic design which was the purpose of my visit. Not that my mind was on graphics, but being as that was what I was being paid for I did feel that I ought to at least mention it some time during the day.

The extra effort of that day's work was about the final nail in the proverbial coffin. I knew that I should have cancelled it but I didn't and I regretted it. Although I'd taken the train and had avoided the boredom and monotony of the 150-mile drive, I arrived home in a miserable, confused state. All I wanted to do was sleep, but the idea was out of the question. I was beginning to think that I'd blown it. Too much.

Saturday, October 17, 1 mile. During the morning I made an attempt at a run round the hill. I did not feel at all like running. I felt weaker than at any time during the past six months. My head was behaving as if I had a hangover from too much to drink which was impossible. My body just felt a wreck. People who passed me in the street commented on how ill I looked and asked whether there was anything wrong.

It was foolish even to try to go anywhere really, and by the time I reached the end of the High Street I knew it for a fact. I just could not run. I was incapable of running anywhere, any distance. I tried to walk a little and then run a little, but it just didn't work. My body had just packed up completely and wouldn't do anything.

Walking back to the house was excruciatingly painful. By now Pat was alarmed and genuinely concerned about my state of health, and there was little that I could do or say that could alleviate the fear that, after all this, there was a strong possibility that we were not going anywhere. She really was having to put up with a hell of a lot.

I took a long bath and did not know what I could or should do. Any thought of going to London tomorrow was out and even trying to do my last long training run locally seemed doubtful. After an hour in the hot soapy suds I crawled down and sat in front of the television at about 11.30 and I didn't move. I half-slept and half-worried my way through the whole of the day, eventually drifting off into a restless, fretful sleep at about 10.00.

Sunday, October 18. Today, Sunday, was a repeat of Saturday. I got out of bed about 10.00 and had breakfast made for me and brought to my invalid's commode in front of the fire.

I stayed there all day. My head and body were in such a state of shock that I had little idea as to how I was going to get myself back together. I felt that I had to make one final effort to do my last long run, but knew that it was physically impossible. If I could just find the energy to push myself, just this one last time, then I could pack it in for the next week and take whatever turned up in my stride.

So I simply sat there and wondered, like an ailing geriatric, with a chequered rug around my knees, and had the three meals of the day brought to me by concerned members of my family who, having left the food, returned quickly to the kitchen for pleasanter company.

Mum and Dad arrived during the evening to begin the 'looking after the kids whilst Pat and I were in New York' period. I think they were more than a little horrified by the sight of their son and heir all wrapped up on the sofa as if suffering from an attack of something nasty. I had lost at least a stone in weight since I had last seen them some three months before, and although theoretically reasonably physically fit, I looked horribly drawn and hollow-cheeked. My friendly cuddly tummy had gone completely and my mother spent the best part of the evening extracting a promise from me that I wouldn't do another marathon as long as I lived.

Tomorrow I must find the energy from somewhere to do

a 15-mile run, but I just have no idea where to look for it.

Monday, October 19, 16 miles. I think that I had recovered a little over the weekend. My 48 hours of doing nothing but sitting in front of the log fire, drinking milky coffee and generally feeling sorry for myself had done me nothing but good. Not that I felt like running; the very thought of it still made me weak at the knees, but I was at least able to handle the thought, whereas before I had dismissed the idea out of hand.

My last day at college had been very similar to the previous week — more or less a disaster. I was only too pleased to leave the place and its people at 4.00. But the reality was that today was the last day that I could attempt the 15 or so miles that I felt I had to do before leaving for New York. I reluctantly drove home, not knowing what I was letting myself in for.

I acknowledged the family group and went upstairs. After some ten minutes I reappeared in my tracksuit and went back outside into the falling darkness, but the rain began to come down in bucketfuls and I quickly returned to put on the waterproof oversuit. The season was one of lost summer and approaching winter, grey and sad. The state of the weather filled my head with terrible thoughts of disaster. Trying to run on such a night, what if I should pull a muscle or twist a knee? I eventually managed to force my way out of the house again and down Riverside towards the Old Pier.

I had little idea as to what would happen. The thoughts of the disaster of Saturday and the weekend spent in my 'comfy' chair did nothing to encourage me. But I had to try to run, even if I was to be eventually carted home in a plastic bag. To my relief, the run was easier than Saturday's; the rest had done me good and I began to enjoy the feeling of restored health and the rain on my face. I could feel my temperature zooming upwards with the effects of the plastic oversuit, and before I had covered 3 miles, I was as wet inside as out.

I had spent the first 3 or 4 miles deciding exactly where I was going to run. I felt that I needed somewhere a little spectacular, somewhere that was appropriate for the last of my long training runs. Woodspring Priory was the place, along the headland — the furthest point. There seemed to be some reasoning in that, some sort of defiant gesture, I suppose. Along the top with the sea on both sides and the rain and the wind blasting all around.

By the time I reached Sand Bay the wind had grown stronger and I tightened the blue rainsuit around my middle and neck, eventually pulling on the head cover which had the effect of cutting out the sound and touch of the wind, sea and rain. Once I'd reached the foot of the headland at the far end of Sand Bay I followed the path that leads up the side until I'd reached the top. Then along the ridge I sped as the last signs of light began to disappear, and the grey and dark blue of the night spread across the waters and the hills in the distance. It was an easy run from there to the end, slightly downhill towards the rocks and the swirling waters of a fast receding tide.

Once there, I stopped. I said hello to a solitary rabbit who did not reply, but made a speedy exit into a convenient gorse bush. Then I bade the Bristol Channel a fond farewell. I stayed for a short while, about the length of time it took to embed the memory of that dark and blowy night firmly in my head.

'See you when I get back,' I said, and lifted both arms high above my head. 'That's No. 2 memory for New York.' And I turned and began the climb back up to the high point of the headland and the comparative calm and shelter of the path back to the beach.

The run home was not successful by any measure that you may care to take to it. I had been sweating profusely for the last two hours and my thick woollen tracksuit was wringing wet. It made running even more difficult than usual, rather like trying to move with your legs tied together. Soon the pleasure of the outward journey was replaced with some concern as to how I was going to get home. The wind and rain had not let up for one moment and I could feel what energy and self will I had left rapidly failing. My legs were unable to lift themselves off the ground, and instead of being able to run I began to shuffle along the watery paths and muddy roads that lead up and away from the beach.

At Worle, still with 4 miles to go, I gave up any idea I might have had of running the full distance home. It was now about seven o'clock, the weather was still foul, and there seemed few options open to me. I think I cast out the one about calling for Pat to come and collect me partly because of her concern about the state of my health and her belief that I had gone completely over the top, but I also felt that I *had* to get round on this, the last of my great efforts before New York; if I gave up on this one, I might give up in the real thing. I felt, too, that I still had some energy left, and if that was true, the least that I could do would be to keep on moving, even if it was at walking pace. It was a continuation of the old battle between not wanting to give up and not wanting to push myself too far: I didn't know whereabouts on that scale I was.

My inability to decide whether to continue or not meant that I half-walked and half-ran the remaining distance in a most unsatisfactory way and arrived home some three hours after I had set off. I was exhausted. I cannot ever remember feeling so tired, mentally or physically. I had no energy, no awareness of what had just happened, that I had just completed six months of training, that all I had to do now was to get to New York and run. I lay in a state of collapse for some considerable time in the hot bath. Then I weighed myself: 10 stone 12 lbs. I could hardly believe it. I hadn't been that weight since I was about seventeen. I had lost over a stone and a half since the beginning of June and it came as a bit of a shock to the system. What exactly was I doing to my body? How much more was it capable of taking? It was true that I had needed to lose weight, get rid of some of the beer paunch. But a stone and a half!

My concern for the state of my health soon began to be overshadowed by the knowledge that I had done everything that I set out to do. I knew that I now had no control over what happened in New York and it was therefore silly to give the idea too much head room. Assuming that I could survive this present crisis, I was as fit as I was ever going to be and I wasn't suffering from pulled, strained or torn ligaments or muscles, or any illness that would lay me low for the marathon. I had managed the self-imposed abstinence from booze, having not touched a drop for two months. I had disappeared from the social calendar, bringing forth comments such as 'Oh, he's really boring now that he's taken up marathon running' and 'Oh, him — yes he used to be a lot of fun. Do you remember what's-his-name?'

But I had done it. Thank God. It was as if I had actually finished the marathon itself — an intense feeling of relief and pleasure. I knew that most of the worry and tension was over, that there was nothing else that I was capable of doing to make myself fitter or healthier, and I resolved to begin a sort of countdown to next Sunday, a 'start enjoying it, Rob' programme.

Half an hour later saw me down in the Bell with Pat, Mum and Dad, plus a large plateful of steak and chips and my first bottle of Guinness since August. Before an hour was up I had consumed three more and felt better than I had done for several weeks. The worst bit was over. Tomorrow we leave for New York.

Part Three

New York

Chapter Fourteen

Arrival in New York. I survey the marathon route. I collect my running number. Filming recommences. The Breakfast Run.

Tuesday, October 20. The flight over was enjoyable, although leaving the kids at home was as difficult as it always is. We'd been delayed on the runway for nearly 3 hours at Heathrow, which every one of the 200 runners on board could well have done without. It was something to do with some nuts and bolts coming undone on the wing, so rumour had it.

During the flight I was able to drive the Air India 747 for a short distance — well, not exactly, but I did get up on to the flight deck and have a chat to the pilots, who certainly gave the impression that they knew what they were doing even if they didn't. There were free gin and tonics in the company of the chief steward, a quick glimpse of the film, several platefuls of curry and cakes, and we had arrived at Kennedy.

The hotel was as one would expect in the centre of New York — a large ugly building of thirty floors nestling on 43rd and 8th Avenue. Our room was on the twenty-fourth floor and gave fine views across the Hudson River and beyond into New Jersey.

This was not my first trip to New York. In fact I had worked in New York State for a year during the early 70s and had made the odd pilgrimage to the Big Apple. I had also returned two years before to play an away skittles match for a local pub, but that's another story. I was therefore familiar with the habits and local customs of the New Yorkers, but the first burger and coke of the trip presented us with more than enough memories of a typical American hamburger joint to last for the full seven days.

Wednesday, October 21. Although I had not expected to take the trip around the course, as offered by our travel organisers who had exported the job lot of assorted talent over to the States, I decided that it would be no bad thing to do some sort of survey so as to 'suss' out likely filming spots with Paul and Nick. We also had the time difference working in our favour, which meant that getting up at a reasonable time wasn't too difficult.

So after breakfast we took the Greyhound bus round the 26-mile course. It certainly seemed a long way, beginning on Staten Island, crossing the huge Verrazano Narrows Bridge and into Brooklyn. The course had already been marked out on the road, a long dotted blue line winding its way through the featureless streets of Brooklyn and on into the featureless streets of Queens, up endless inclines and through potholes full of water or rubbish or both, past broken-down battered cars and side streets full of old black men and wild kids.

On through Queens we went, over the 59th Street Bridge and into Manhattan, down 1st Avenue and into the Bronx; then back into Manhattan through Harlem. What a hell of a long way that was. It had taken us 5 hours to drive it, although we had stopped for an hour or so for lunch.

Once back, we registered at the Sheraton Hotel: memories of registering for the London Marathon at the Strand Palace in March. This time I handed in my registration number and watched as some extremely clever computer printed out my running number, 9982. Then came the goody bag — lots of items such as shorts, T-shirt, sweatbands, posters: a pleasant surprise and very useful. I also collected the running gear which had been put aside for me by Reebok in London, superb running shorts and a string-vest-type running shirt.

On the way out I was accosted by some glamorous lady TV interviewer who insisted on asking stupid questions like 'Has marathon running altered your life?', 'Is it a mentally and spiritually rewarding experience?' and 'Why do you run marathons?', none of which I felt capable of answering and my flippant replies did little to amuse her. She smiled her make-up at me and went on her search for a more interesting and talkative subject. I suppose she was after some great truth or other, but I certainly could not supply her with one. God alone knew what I was doing there! Writing a book might wrench the reasons out of me, but 10 seconds of TV time didn't stand a chance.

During the evening we saw 'Chariots of Fire' which seemed the most appropriate film possible. Relaxing there and in the restaurant later was the perfect thing to do in order to remove the pictures of the marathon route which had been well etched into my memory.

Thursday, October 22. Apart from the fire in the hotel and the fact that we had to evacuate the building at 3.30 in the morning, I passed a peaceful night, sleeping well, and even felt like a little light exercise before breakfast. So up 8th Avenue to Central Park I trotted, along with the other 1000 or so runners who seemed to be cluttering up the streets. The sight of tracksuited runners on Broadway, all aiming for the park, was an incongruous one.

Central Park was full of people riding, running, jogging, skating with headsets and singing to themselves as they drifted past in a world of their own. The grey squirrels, outnumbering the runners, darted across the paths and up into the trees which were overshadowed by the tall buildings surrounding the park. The stands, or bleachers, were still being erected at the finishing line and the New York Road Runners' Club caravan with all the various press exchanges stood to one side. The blue dotted line came to an abrupt stop and I stood on it for several minutes, watching as the rest of the world ran by and thinking how pleased I'd be to see that point on Sunday.

I spent the rest of the day idly — and visiting bars and clubs — before an early night.

Friday, October 23. The first day of filming in New York. The crew arrived at about 8.30 and we met in the hotel lobby as one tends to do on such occasions. They were Dave the camera, Mike the camera assistant and Stuart the sound: three good men and true who were doing their three-month secondment in New York from the BBC in London.

We did various shots, running up 43rd and down 7th, under trucks and passing yellow cabs. We filmed on Broadway and 5th Avenue, then moved into Central Park where hundreds of runners were all taking exercise in the sanest part of New York City. We even managed to disturb some shady deal which was taking place beneath one of the many bridges: as our cameras came on to the scene, the half-dozen Italian-looking men in dark suits and knee-length overcoats faded into obscurity.

Then I ran straight into Tom Courtney who just happened to be walking through. Astounded, I plucked up the courage to ask him if he'd mind doing a quick walk-through shot, and he seemed happy to do it. So you could say that I've appeared in a film with Tom Courtney and there aren't many of us who can say that! If it doesn't come out, I think I'll cry.

A heavy downpour of rain washed out any further prospect of filming for the day and, following a more than pleasant lunch at Rosie O'Grady's, we packed up and returned to the hotel. There we all stayed until the evening and, with thoughts of the Breakfast Run the following day, took another early night.

Saturday, October 24, 2 miles. I rose early. It was a lovely day, very cold but beautifully clear.

Again the crew was waiting for us in the lobby and we took the second of the hired Dodge transporters down to the United Nations building for the Breakfast Fun Run, an affair organised for all 3000 of the foreign entrants. It was strange to think of myself as being foreign!

At the start Pat joined in, as did Mark and Jane who had accompanied us to the States, although we lost them after about 10 yards and I think they must have walked the rest of the way. The thousands of us setting off on the 2-mile trip through the deserted streets of Manhattan, with police cars and sirens in full flight to the front and to the sides, made an unbelievable sight. To look at us you'd think that we'd been given the presidential escort — and all this for a motley collection of runners who had each probably undergone the same harrowing training programme as myself and who had probably been regarded by his or her respective neighbours as being slightly potty. The run was followed by a great breakfast in Central Park and more 'goody' T-shirts for memories.

During the afternoon we took the helicopter flight over the

city. It was an astonishing experience, the first time that I'd ever been in a helicopter and the sight of Manhattan below on a crystal-clear afternoon is a memory I'll never forget. At least you couldn't see the 'garbage' from up there, floating over the Statue of Liberty with the shadow of the aircraft on the water below, where the Hudson and East Rivers meet.

That evening there was a pasta party and a great 'eat in' — pasta for the carbohydrates, along with several cans of good beer. Then it was back to the hotel, with nothing to do now but reach for the indigestion tablets.

Chapter Fifteen

Race Day comes at last.

Sunday, October 25. I slept well, considering what my poor confused brain must have been going through, trying to find a way of putting together an odd assortment of thoughts and emotions. My early-morning call came at 6.15 and was unnecessary by some 25 minutes: I had awakened to the sound of car horns and the sirens of police cars which replace the dawn chorus in New York City. The light was beginning to find its way through the two layers of curtaining to expose the hideous paper which covered the walls of the hotel bedroom. I didn't seem to feel tired. At least the changed hour back to standard time was working for and not against me, as it had in the London Marathon in March just six months before. At least some of the gods were on my side.

I performed the usual scratching shuffle to the window and stared out at the odd mixture of vernacular architecture, gridded streets and tall buildings, the docks and the Hudson River beyond. And further still the New Jersey shore and skyline. The day was clear and sunny with small white clouds floating above the layer of light brown mist, the result of yesterday's traffic pollution which hadn't had time to settle or blow away. The forecast had been for a dull, grey, fairly warm morning with light showers in the afternoon. It sounded about as good as one could have hoped for, and certainly better than the brilliant sunshine of the previous day or the torrential rain of the one before that when the heavens opened and the rain fell and nothing could be seen of any of the tall buildings above the twelfth floor. Then the neon lights of Times Square and Broadway were reflected back off the wet streets, and the dips and hollows which were called roads filled up with water and gave the car and cab drivers a new game to play with pedestrians.

My running gear was already laid out at the bottom of the

bed. I had set it out the previous evening, rather in the manner of stockings or a pillow case on Christmas Eve. I began filling them with me in the same way as I remember watching Dave Frances doing in the hotel room just before the London Marathon. I also performed the ritual which has to accompany it: the smearing of Vaseline on the feet and ankles, the donning of the socks, neatly rolled up, without any raised seams to rub on the inside of the shoes, the putting on of the clean green pants, specially brought all the way from Sainsbury's for this purpose, and the Bill Rogers running shorts and vest which I had collected from the Reebok stand at the Sheraton Center. Then it all had to be taken off again to allow for 10 minutes' soak in a hot tub. I had found that mornings were the one time of the day when you could guarantee that there wouldn't be any hot water, but at 6.15 I thought that I might 'beat the cistern', so to speak, and I did.

This time, for this marathon, there was nobody to offer advice about what to do and how to do it. No other person in the room who could say that they had 'done it loads of times before' and that it wasn't really all that hard and that I should get round without any problems. There was just little old me, sitting in a bath tub looking down at my little budgie feet, wondering if they had enough character in them to take me round 26 miles of New York tarmac.

So I made do. Embrocation was applied to the legs until the smell made Pat get out of bed to open the window. I must confess that the stench was pretty bad: I had almost asphyxiated my fellow passengers in the lift with it a few days earlier.

The preparation continued. After the embrocation I applied plasters to my nipples (making sure to wash my hands well before doing so) and repeated the Vaseline procedure on my feet, legs and arms. I put on the running shoes in which I had done most of my training and tied them carefully in a double knot. My running number was already fixed firmly to my vest with five safety pins. I sat on the bed and looked at myself in the mirror above the dressing table. Even if I wasn't a particularly good runner, at least I could have been mistaken for one. Anyone who has travelled 3500 miles for a race and looks like that can't be that bad. Thank God for first impressions!

It was time for the cover-up. So I put on the grey sweatsuit, took the plastic rainsuit out of my running bag, had a last quick look at the boats moving along the Hudson River and went down to breakfast. On the way, the lift was full of runners, all standing bolt upright and expressionless, rather like a box of Russian dolls. 'Room for two more?' I asked as Pat and I squeezed our way in. Not a lot of answers came back to me, so I deduced that either the lift was full of non-English-speaking peoples or that they were all deep in prayer as their hands were firmly clasped together. But then it is difficult to know what to do with hands in a full lift.

All that could be heard was the creaking of the winding gear as we descended the twenty-three floors, stopping at each to collect, reject or eject ingredients of the incongruous mixture of people. There was none of the suited, briefcased variety of person on an expense account which one normally associates with hotel lifts, but instead a shabby, tatty group of pensive, gaunt athletes, each one thinking the same sort of thoughts, a combination of high expectation and 'What the hell am I doing here?' Down in the lobby was a similar array of brightly coloured tracksuits, odd woolly jumpers and expensive running shoes, while a fierce odour of liniment overpowered the smell of bacon, scrambled eggs, ham and coffee which percolated from the large dining room into the foyer.

'Cutting it a bit fine, aren't you?' said the travel lady who had organised our charabanc from London. It was well past seven o'clock and the last of the chartered buses were already beginning to leave the hotel to ferry the runners to the Lincoln Center where more chartered buses were ferrying them out to the start of the race on Staten Island.

'I'm going with the BBC crew,' I answered in a voice which sought to be authoritative, firm and a trifle rebuking, but which came out more than a little timid and weak and half an octave higher than normal.

'Are you sure that they will be allowed into Fort Wadsworth? As far as I know no one but runners can get in.'

More doubts. Something else to worry about. Why couldn't she have just wished me good luck or 'Have a nice day' or some other friendly greeting instead of filling my head with sad thoughts of me, standing outside the gates of heaven, watching as the privileged few, all 16,000 of them, set off on their run to glory.

'Press passes,' I thought. 'Press passes,' I said and reassured doubting 'Fiona' and myself with one phrase.

It had been crowded during the week but this was like the departure lounge at Heathrow Airport except that none of us was going to be 'carried away on silver wings'. The only carrying away about to take place was that done by our little old feet. And knowing the doubt and fear that each one of us felt about the airworthiness of these nether portions of the body, the foyer resembled Heathrow departure lounge in more ways than one.

At breakfast, my appetite vanished as I sat at the table with Pat, Mark and Jane and watched as the BBC crew arrived through the large dining-room door. I was half way through a large mouthful of home-fries at the time. I pushed the plate away and resorted to the black coffee and fruit juice. When that had gone there was nothing else for me to resort to and I stood up, wished each of them one last 'Have a nice day in the bleachers', picked up my goody bag and joined Paul, Nick and the crew in the lobby.

We quit the hotel. There were still a few runners left in the lobby, though the place was a shadow of what it had been some 30 minutes before. Outside the day was still bright — not that it is all that easy to tell what sort of day it is from ground level in New York as the shadows and winds caused by the sky-scrapers can confuse the senses. But what sky could be seen contained a few more white clouds, way up beyond the tops of the buildings, than had been there at first light.

The new driver and the third vehicle in as many days were waiting outside the hotel. The crew had insisted that the van-hire company supply a more knowledgeable driver and a better-sprung van than those supplied the previous day. That combination had shaken the flesh from our bones and the film from the cameras as we felt a large percentage of the holes which make up the streets of New York City.

Paul the producer sat nervously in the back of the blue and light grey Dodge van, mumbling things to himself like an apprehensive bridegroom. I could understand why, for if this particular marriage did not work out within the next 5 hours, his own back in England might undergo severe pressure as the flak from the BBC in Bristol ricocheted around his head. So many things could go so horribly wrong, and keeping our combined fingers crossed and trusting in Paul's lucky Cornish pixie, which he carried around with him at all times, were about the best deterrents any of us could think of.

'Have you got your running number, Rob?'

'Yes Paul.'

'And your registration number?'

'Don't need it.'

'Are you sure? I mean, don't you think it would be a good idea to have it just in case?'

'No Paul, that was only needed to get me this running number.' And I lifted up the tracksuit top and my grey sweater to show him the piece of paper pinned to my vest.

'Well, if you *are* sure, Rob but if you're not, we could always go back and get it before we go any further ... '

Nothing I could do would have really reassured him at that stage, apart from going back to the hotel and removing the entire contents of my room, just in case any one of the items was needed.

It was as quiet inside the van as it was outside. Certainly this was in contrast to the incessant horns and sirens which usually filled the air every hour of both day and night. But at about 7.30 on that Sunday morning they seemed to have given way to what few indigenous sounds there were left in Times Square and on Broadway.

We left Manhattan via the Brooklyn Bridge, joining the Belt

Parkway which runs along the outside of Brooklyn. This is a sort of dual carriageway in both senses of the word, a dodgem-cum-stockcar track where no one knows the rules and the Highway Code has as much relevance to driving on it as a *Cordon Bleu* cookery book has in a hamburger joint. Today, however, as a gift to the rest of the world from the people of Brooklyn, it was almost empty and we drove the 5 miles to the Verrazano Narrows Bridge with no more than a couple of near misses from passing trucks and a few Sunday morning mild obscenities delivered to stationary cars and pedestrians, many of whose ancestors had made the great journey across the seas only to become permanently embedded in the fast-failing tarmac.

A large road sign proclaiming that we were approaching the 'Last Entry to Brooklyn' struck a literary chord somewhere and we arrived at the lower level of the bridge. Its top layer of six lanes had already been closed to traffic some hours before. This had been achieved by placing a huge gritting truck across the width of the three approaching lanes and surrounding it with a pleasant assortment of police cars with pretty red and orange flashing lights, a sight which I could see from a distance of some three-quarters of a mile but which the driver of a Lancia clearly had not as the wreckage of his motor car gave proof.

From the bridge I looked back to my right to the views of Manhattan in the hazy distance. What a hell of a long way to run, even in a straight line, let alone by way of this magical mystery tour through Brooklyn, Queens, Bronx, and back to Manhattan through Harlem. Just to the left of Manhattan the Statue of Liberty, green against the blue-grey of the water, held high in her right hand the mighty torch of freedom, which from my position looked horribly like a giant starting pistol.

Once at the far side, I had 'arrived'. I felt a wonderful sense of relief at getting there, just to the starting line. So many things could have gone wrong over the previous six months. The arrangements to do with the travel alone were complicated enough, to say nothing of the training, the swollen ankles, the risk of going down with something nasty a week or two before I left or, even worse, of catching some 'foreign ailment' after reaching New York — I had spent a lift journey from the third to the twenty-fourth floor holding my breath after a fellow passenger had sneezed! This feeling of paranoid hypochondria had been my constant companion for so many weeks now that as it left me on that Sunday morning in October, it was rather like waving goodbye to an old friend on a dark and chilly railway platform. Fortunately the relief of arriving safely acted as a sort of balance to the tension which I felt about the race.

The place was full. Between the end of the bridge and the row of turnpikes the scene was one of beautiful chaos: police on bikes and in cars, trying to keep the traffic flowing; buses arriving full from Manhattan being quickly unloaded and returned to the Lincoln Center to fill up with more runners: ABC camera crews, as ubiquitous as the police, came in specially designed cars with open backs and the cameras on giro heads sticking out at the rear. There were three such vans in sight, plus a crew at the top of a large crane, hovering up and down over the heads of the crowds below. And as if this were not enough, two ABC helicopters buzzed back and forth overhead making circles around the Goodyear blimp as it droned its way about in an awkward bumbly sort of way, back and forth between Staten Island and Manhattan.

A fairground organ blew and sucked its way through a series of 'Dixie melodies'. Officials in bright yellow cagoules rushed to and fro with bits of paper or bits of runners. Chaos, beautiful chaos. And in the middle of it all marched the Band of the US Marines, playing martial music, giving the illusion of organisation to the proceedings.

Where there was space left by the mixture of law-and-order and media men, there were runners. Millions and millions of us, swarming about like brightly coloured honey bees, off the buses and into Fort Wadsworth, looking for the enrolment tent, for the marathon, and not for the US Army whose land it was.

I left the tarmac and the flatness of the road and moved along with others, through the specially erected 'hole' in the fence and into Fort Wadsworth, past officials giving a preliminary glance at our running numbers to assure themselves that we were legitimate, and on into the registration tent. There was no queueing; a quick stripe with the light pen on my computer running number and I was checked off and out the other side within a matter of seconds. There was nothing to do but run!

Inside I joined up with the camera crew who were busy filming odd-looking runners asleep under tin foil or standing in excruciatingly painful positions apparently 'limbering up' although there were still a good 2 hours to go to the start of the race. I considered such exercises to be a little premature; how people could keep that sort of discomfort up for 2 hours and then run a marathon was beyond me. I was yet to flex a muscle in anger and I was determined to keep it that way for as long as possible. I was convinced that I would have quite enough exercise before the day was through without beginning before it was absolutely necessary.

At that point the park looked as if it was preparing for a yoga convention with people doing disgusting things up against trees or each other. There was a group of runners, who appeared to be representing a national team, parading up and down singing away in something that sounded vaguely Italian. Smaller groups of club runners were jogging to this point and then back to that point as if they were undergoing the final phases of a well co-ordinated training schedule. 'Three gals from Texas', claimed one song. A banner lent support to 'Mabel, Sibyll, Wendy and Bert'. 'Lucky Bert,' thought I. And various random groups attempted to alleviate tension by singing songs about overcoming this and that.

I drifted aimlessly around the park, finding the coffee truck which contained some twenty large chromium-plated tea dispensers. Black coffee, white coffee, black with sugar, white with sugar, tea, hot chocolate with the same list of permutations that the coffee had. I chose black coffee. Bad as it was, it tasted good. I saw Russell, a friend from London, sitting peacefully on the grass to one side of the coffee truck and went over for a natter. It was reassuring to see him there. As he had done the race last year, it was good to be able to ask someone what it was like on the 'other side' of the bridge. He sounded confident and happy and not a bit up-tight. We decided to run the first few miles together and then see what happened. For me, I thought it likely that I would do most of the run on my own, but to have someone else there at the start would be comforting. We wished each other well and arranged to meet at the 3-hour marker at the start, something which sounded so ridiculously easy that it didn't merit a second thought.

I strolled around. There wasn't a great deal of filming to be done, just the odd shot of sitting against this pole, or drinking some of the energy-replacement drink ERD, the taste of which always comes as a bit of a shock. There was the usual assortment of runners in fancy dress. Batman or Lucifer, I'm not sure which, Computer Man, Green Man, a bloke from Birmingham College of Food and Technology wearing a Union Jack and carrying a frying pan — apparently the fool intended to run like this, flipping a pancake. There were two men in wheelchairs and a guy with a wooden leg had apparently just left on an early start to get round before the light began to fade.

Overhead the blimp was still playing 'Ring Around the Helicopters' and on a higher level, above them both, the transatlantic Jumbos could be seen flying slowly and quietly into Kennedy and La Guardia.

The two hours passed, evenly interspaced by nervous visits to one of the hundreds of specially erected 'Rent-a-Johns'. They seemed innumerable and resembled the rows of beach huts found at popular seaside resorts. And on the far side of the park was the fine, well-documented construction of timber and polythene some 50 yards long which accommodated the immediate needs of the males. During one such visit I met up with another friend, John, and we chatted as we queued. What an odd place to hold a conversation about Bristol and mutual friends!

Paul suggested a quick interview to camera, a 'How do you feel now?' sort of thing, and I had to grope around for something to say. I think at that point the most accurate account of my feelings would have been a long blank stare at

126

the lens. But it was soon over and the crew made their way out of the registration area and into the bridge to find a suitable position for filming the start of the run. I arranged to meet them at the 3.00 mark just before the start, partially so that they could do a quick shot of me lining up and partially to hand them my tracksuit.

With 30 minutes to go before blast off we began to evacuate Fort Wadsworth. I cannot remember hearing instructions telling us to make our way to the start but we all did, rather like the way in which cows move slowly towards the gate in the corner of the field around milking time. Within a few minutes we were all gathered in the same corner of the park, by the hole in the fence, standing like turkeys at Christmas, clucking to each other with that total ignorance and lack of awareness of what the next few hours would hold.

The traffic was eventually halted on the bridge, and we surged forward on to the eight-lane freeway. I found Russell.

'The first few miles, then.'

'Great. Best of luck, Rob.'

'And you, Russell. Have a good run.'

But there was no sign of Paul or the crew. And there was I, the only one of the 16,000 runners still wearing a tracksuit. Good start, I thought, missing the crew right at the beginning. If we can't meet up when I'm standing still how the hell are we going to do it when I'm on the move?

The runners still continued to pour out from the park, filling the various estimated time slots which expanded far beyond what they were capable of doing, and eventually bursting over the tarmac so that the intended long line of bodies waiting at the start must have resembled an enormous pear from above. And the Band of the Marines, who up until recently had been playing away on the sidelines, found themselves contenders for a 2.45 marathon.

I tried to stay on the outside, as arranged for filming, and quickly lost sight of Russell and the park, Staten Island, Manhattan and the rest of the world. I was cocooned in a warm mixture of runners wearing a collection of clothing that looked

127

as if it had all come from the Salvation Army — any old thing that could be discarded along the route as the body began to object to the heat and the sweat.

With some 2 or 3 minutes left and still no sign of the crew, I took off my tracksuit, wondering what the hell to do with it. I found a bag on the floor and stuffed the suit and my sweater into it. Just behind me a lady was saying fond farewells to two men wearing policemen's helmets. She turned out to be from Derbyshire Constabulary and I entrusted the bag to her without much thought as to whether or not I would see it all again. The first cock-up.

There was just time for one last pee among the hedges at the side of the road. Where does it all come from? 'One minute left,' boomed from the loudspeakers, and I felt like I needed another. But as this was just not physically possible, I stayed put and jumped up and down instead.

During the last few seconds I thought of Banwell and the kids at home and how excited they must be feeling, of Pat, Mark and Jane at the finish, listening to the announcement of the start on the speakers and how horrible this was going to be for them. And of the camping holiday in Cornwall and that morning run along the cliff tops with the gulls and guillemots and the small white fishing boats way out in the distance and the quiet of Killigerran Head.

Chapter Sixteen

Where's the camera crew?

The 105 mm Howitzer let forth a monstrous boom and lashings of smoke some 30 yards in front. I let forth a great shout of hope and expectation, crossed the start line within a few seconds and began the 1981 New York Marathon.

It was a marvellous feeling actually to be running at last. There were no worries about fitness or tiredness, just a sense of relief and enjoyment. But the nagging anxiety about missing the film crew came back at the foot of the bridge. It really was important that they get this part somehow and yet they were nowhere to be seen. Thoughts of cock-up number two loomed over me, as did the form of the Verrazano Bridge, and where I had expected them to be they were not. Missing me during the middle of the race was one thing, but making a film about the New York Marathon without a beginning or an end seemed a little absurd. We had made arrangements: I would wave a white scarf and Paul a white card with 'BBC' written on it. How could we possibly fail to see each other, we had said. At that point in the race there seemed to be 15,000 people waving white scarves and most spectators were holding up bits of white board with something or other written on them.

I had moved about ¼ mile up on to the bridge when I saw them. I was running, as agreed, on the left of the right carriage-way, in the centre of the bridge. They had promised to be in the middle somewhere. But they were not. As I looked over to the far right, whom should I see but the four of them, gazing back towards the start like homesick sailors leaving port. Between me and them were several thousand runners moving at a steady 10 knots. Beyond them was the Atlantic Ocean and the shore-line of England. And from where I was, it seemed about as impossible for me to get to them as it would have been to reach the shores of Cornwall. To shout would have been appallingly stupid but as there was nothing else I could do I yelled my head off. It had the effect that I knew it would and the four sideways faces moved not an inch. For me to stop would have been as dangerous as falling at Bechers Brook. So I began the slow 'tack' to the right across the unstoppable sea of legs. After some 500 yards and a similar number of abusive words from many of the other runners I hit the right-hand side of the bridge and began the experience of being the first man to run the New York Marathon in the opposite direction. I made my way slowly back on the narrow pavement and tapped Paul on the shoulder.

'Coo-ee, are you looking for me?'

'Oh, thank God you're here, Rob, just go back to the start and run up towards us will you?'

Why don't we just stop the race and begin it all over again, I thought. I was sure old Salazar wouldn't mind and we could easily load up the cannon again!

I went backwards still further and leapt back into the madding crowd, past the camera as if it wasn't there, and made for the top of the bridge. God, I hoped I wouldn't have to do that all the way round.

From that high point, Manhattan, with the finish buried somewhere deep amongst its tall buildings, could be seen in the distance. What an extraordinarily long way away it looked. Perhaps that was what Hamlyn looked like to all those children and, come to think of it, I could still hear the band playing in the distance.

One mile out was the first casualty. A man with a badly pulled leg muscle was being propped up against the superstructure. What a terrible disappointment for him — to do all that work, all that training and not even make the far side of the bridge.

I passed off the bridge and into Brooklyn and sight of the first real crowds, just as I remembered London at the entrance to Greenwich Park. There were thousands and thousands of them, all shouting and cheering, and I doubt if there was a single runner who didn't feel a quickening of pace as we left the spiralling exit roads of the Verrazano Bridge and moved on to the pot-holed thoroughfares of Brooklyn.

I suppose I was bound to compare the two marathons, London and New York, just as on the London run I had had to rely on what little experience I had gained during the training runs around Banwell. The miles seemed to be going much more quickly here and I remember being surprised at seeing the large blue 4-mile marker coming up on the road between the well-heeled feet of the runners in front.

Brooklyn and 4th Avenue were about as straight and as long as London had been winding and narrow. It was the first of the long straights: 6 miles long without so much as a hint to port or a waver to starboard. The road itself, or rather what one could see of it through the embedded bottle tops and beer-can rip caps, resembled a disused airstrip. My feet went right down at one moment and at another stumbled on a ridge created by the hot sun and some stationary car.

The two running groups, red and blue, had not yet come together and at that point were running side by side down both sides of the carriageway, separated by a 6-mile strip of red tape, tied at intervals to large wooden barriers. On either side and down the central reservation stood people shouting encouragement, hands held outstretched, slapping the hands of the runners as they moved past and picking up what was written on their shirts.

'Right, right. All right.'

'Go, 9982.'

'Move it, Reebok.'

'You're lookin' good, real good.'

And I always seemed to know who was coming up behind or running alongside as cries of 'Run on, Betty' or 'Go, go, 7684' constantly accompanied the sounds of the running feet on the dry tarmac.

I began drinking water at the second station. 'Take a little often' had worked in London so I didn't see why I should change my drinking habits. My two-month period of abstinence was enough for any man.

At 8 miles I caught sight of the crew, this time on the left. After the previous miles and thousands of different faces, it was like meeting old friends. As sure as eggs were eggs, nobody else in Brooklyn knew me and it was great to see them, this little band of roaming media men, poking their respective cameras, mikes, clapper boards and notices into the air. As soon as I saw them I began flourishing the white scarf in the air, not knowing if they had seen me or not. I saw Paul's arm with the card move in acknowledgement and I dropped the scarf and stuffed it back inside my shorts. I was sorry that I couldn't turn round to them and have a quick chat or smile, so I ran past with a blank expression which covered a chuckle. Once past, with the camera at the back of my head, I let out a laugh and a shout at getting the second of our five shots over with. I wondered whose relief was the greatest, and I thought of their rush to the Queensborough Bridge and that kept me amused for the next mile. At least my route ahead was clear — or relatively so if you excluded the 8,000 or 9,000 runners who were in between me and the finishing line.

A well-concealed fire truck down one of the side streets revealed its presence with its hydraulic ladders which were projecting over 4th Avenue like an inquisitive giraffe. Banners hanging from its neck gave visual support to 'Andy and Bill' from the 5th Precinct and the four bodies in the turret in full gear filled in with the verbal.

At the end of 4th Avenue the thin red tape finished, and the two groups joined together and we all 'hung a right' into Lafayette Avenue and the first incline. The crowds seemed thicker in number and a whole lot noisier than even those on 4th. There were parties going on on both sides of the streets and in the red and white shingled apartments and front yards. An extremely loud, heavy rock band filled the air with a million decibels and the 'brewery which made Milwaukee famous' was coining a fortune at 11.00 on a Sunday morning. The police, who lined the streets at intervals of about 20 yards on both sides, just smiled and chatted to both runners and spectators. There was so much effort being expended by the crowds that at one point it seemed that the runners were clapping and cheering them as much as they were clapping and cheering us. Perhaps they too had been in training for six months — they certainly looked fit enough.

I was running well and apart from a few odd muscle twinges and the nagging pain in my right ankle, there was nothing wrong with me. I felt happy and confident. I didn't carry a watch and was running much more against myself than against the clock. Apart from the anguish of making the film and hoping that the stuff came out okay after it had been processed, there was nothing else for me to worry about.

Running in this city was one hell of an experience and such a contrast from what I had been used to. If running through the streets of London had been a culture shock after the hills and beaches of Somerset and Avon, New York was a brain transplant. I kept comparing the buildings and the people, and thoughts of Killigerran Head came flooding back into my head, as I had known they would when I was there in the summer. I remembered logging them away as something to think on when I reached New York.

The districts changed quickly. From the predominantly black areas of downtown Brooklyn, the route led through Boroughpark, the largely Hasidic Jewish section. Here there was no shouting and cheering, just a silent tribute or quiet disbelief from the dark-suited, fur-hatted, long-side-haired gentlemen. No clatter, no radios, no bands, just crowds of people observing a phenomenon which was as much outside their culture as theirs was mine. But within a few blocks the area changed again, back came the noise and the cheering and the first sights of the Pulaski Bridge and the 13.1-mile mark. People lined both sides, and should any one of the runners have missed the halfway line painted on the road several hundred voices pointed it out along with a loudspeaker, which gave the time to the nearest second.

'You're halfway, man, and looking so good.'
'If you can read this, you're running too slow.'
'All the way down, man, easy, easy.'

And the halfway mark came and went and felt marvellous.

But then I got confused as to where I was. I thought I was on the Queensborough Bridge not the Pulaski Bridge and that the buildings on the other side were those of Manhattan and that the crew would be waiting for me. On reaching the middle I realised that I was mistaken and that all my arm shaking and whooping towards the crowd must have appeared more than a little unnecessary to those around me, so I did a quick retreat back into my running boots and pretended that it must have been somebody else. Certainly nobody seemed to take it to heart, and conversation between the runners, although not as noticeable to me as in London, could still be heard above the 'Ha buddy, move it, move it' and 'Sweet movement, sweet, sweet movement.'

I was running steadily. I seemed to be passing people rather than dropping backward, which gave me encouragement — or was it a false sense of security?

The oranges held out by the pretty ladies began to appear and were a change from the salty sweetness of the ERD. More signs — 'Dad, we love you' — and my eyes just filled and the views of Queens melted in front of me. So I held out my hand for the next 100 yards and slapped the waiting hands till my fingers tingled and removed thoughts of Banwell.

Then the bridge. The Queensborough Bridge. The original 59th Street Bridge. A giant of a structure like something out of *The Shape of Things to Come*; weird engineering, as if nobody could quite make up their minds what it should look like; a two-parts Meccano and one-part knitting pattern of a bridge with lanes going through the middle and over the top; a two-tiered structuralist's cake with pedestrian walkways on either side. And on the left of this great erection was a soft, fawn stair carpet, running its entire length as protection against the harshness of the surface, a sort of extra-strong chicken wire through which you can see the East River on an outward tide, swirling against the strong base. In the middle is Roosevelt Island with its buildings which bear more resemblance to nineteenth-century Dartmoor than twentieth-century New York.

The lasting impression, however, is that of approaching Manhattan with its high buildings, stretching from far left to far right. Not only was it a clear sign that I had made 16 miles in good time and in good health, but the sight of this island in all its glory raised my pace and spirit to a ludicrous high.

If the crew had managed it, they should be waiting for me at the far side, and as I reached the middle I began to search amongst the waiting millions far in front and below. I began the scarf-waving bit, which must have appeared absurd to those running alongside me as the nearest spectator was still some ½ mile away.

'Probably the heat.'

'Often gets them about the 16-mile mark, you know, the constant thumping rhythm and the tension.'

Thus I gained a few extra yards of space as the runners took a wide berth so as not to be near this demented loony who, for no apparent reason, kept either stopping and running backwards towards the start line, or continually pulling a large white scarf out of his shorts and waving it frantically over and about his head, or cheering at nothing in particular, or whooping and leaping in the middle of bridges when everyone around was trying hard to settle down into some sort of rhythm.

I came to the end of the magic carpet at an enormous speed, totally over the top, more the sort of speed reserved for a 440 or a run down the road at 2 minutes to closing time. Thousands of people shouted and cheered as 59th Street East met 1st Avenue.

The crew, where was the crew? This flag waving was all very well but it did get to you after a while. Not only that, but if they should see me before I saw them, all the film would consist of would be some idiot who ran the New York Marathon waving a white scarf, apparently looking as if he was eyeing up the local talent by the intensity of his studious gaze.

As I turned on to 59th Street East and looked towards the river I saw them: Dave, the cameraman, on top of a step ladder and Paul, the producer, waving his white card — this time *not* with BBC written on it, as all the sound man had apparently been picking up in Brooklyn was the sound of runners going past shouting some tribute or abuse to the BBC. Trusting that I had been spotted, therefore, I moved towards the outside as I turned left on to 1st Avenue. If this film did finally emerge from the vaults of the BBC, I would be noticeable not by my face, running style or garb but as the only person who did not wave at the camera as they ran past.

I took a quick look over my shoulder to see if I had been seen and as the camera was pointing at my back I assumed the best and carried on running. At that point I think I would still have been prepared to stop, turn round and do that bit again, had they missed me. Past the East World Theater I ran, a 'moviehouse for sexually oriented flicks', showing its current feature 'Exhausted'. The crowds were thicker here than anywhere previously passed and the hand slapping, shouting and general repartee began again in earnest: a real 'welcome to New York' along the 3 miles of 1st Avenue.

As the total of miles covered began to grow, so too did the space between the runners. I suddenly began to feel the effects of two hours plus of running. The eternal 'soft shoe shuffle' along the appalling road surface made me concentrate on what was going on at foot level rather than take notice of what the supporters were saying or doing. To ignore the road by waving and cheering back at the people, to make mental notes as to what they looked like or what they were wearing, only to end up face down on 1st Avenue, would have been most irresponsible. So I concentrated on the old 'one two, one two' and began to prepare for the worst.

I could have sworn that 1st Avenue went on for 120 miles. I could not believe that they had got this part right. Had I seen all the runners heading back from whence they had come, or groups of them standing asking some friendly New York cop for directions to Central Park, I would not have been surprised. It seemed endless: rows and rows of people and buildings, looking like an exercise in one-point perspective where the objective is to find the vanishing point. I could see nothing ahead in which to take comfort and although the crowds gave constant support I could feel my senses beginning to fail.

Within the 3 miles of 1st Avenue I went from a fit, happy athlete doing everything right to a jet-lagged visitor to New York who was having difficulty finding his land legs. My mind began to wander and I found it impossible to concentrate on what was going on around as the people and the buildings drifted past.

I tried to compare distances. The eight miles left was equal to the run from my house to the Old Pier at Kewstoke. I thought of the last training run to the end of Woodspring Priory overlooking the Severn estuary, and of my great defiant gesture, arms outstretched, overlooking the murky grey seas of the Bristol Channel. And I thought of *Tess of the D'Urbervilles*. How anyone running a marathon in New York can think of *Tess of the D'Urbervilles* is still more than a little beyond me, but I did. And the more I began to lose myself in thoughts of long ago, the less I noticed what effect the running was having on me.

So this nostalgic high carried me to the end of 1st Avenue and into the Bronx, and it was there that I woke up. I had to move off the road and on to the pavement to cross over the Willis Avenue Bridge, the fourth of the five bridges which were to be crossed during this marathon. To do this I had to leap through the steel girders, off the rubber matting and back on to the 'chicken wire'. I managed the exercise quite well but a woman following who attempted the same quick step crashed uncontrollably down on to the bridge. She was, luckily, unhurt and was quickly helped to her feet by a group of runners following behind. The last I saw of her, she was still running in the right direction.

One large Dodge truck, with its doors wide open and its driver sitting on the front bumper, had the radio commentary for company. As I passed it some deep American voice was describing the scene in Central Park where Allison Roe had just beaten the women's world record by getting round in 2 hours 25 minutes 28 seconds. A large card propped up against the side gave Salazar's time of 2 hours 8 minutes and 13 seconds, another world record. That was a magnificent moment. I had taken part in a race where two world records had been broken. Even though my part in it was infinitely small, it is the 16,000 runners which make the New York Marathon what it is and each one is inextricably linked to the winners. I felt so absurdly proud, not just for myself but for what the event meant to all of us taking part — those with great ability and those with more luck than energy.

The 3rd Avenue Bridge took me back permanently into Manhattan and Harlem, to the tenement blocks to beat all tenement blocks with their zig-zag rusting fire escapes providing some space for kids to play in or for adults to hang washing or just hang about in. But I was now beginning to find it so hard to keep looking up and almost impossible to notice those things which were going on about me. My legs weren't hurting from pulled tendons or strained muscles but they were getting instructions as to what to do from another source. This was only to be expected, however. I had hardly thought that at this stage I would be bouncing along on the crest of a wave. I made a conscious effort to get my heels down on the road first, to avoid becoming flat-footed and doing any of those Egyptian sand dances. If I once got into that way of moving it would be absolute disaster.

Small groups of black people were sitting around on the pavement or standing on steps leading into apartments. 'Go, brother' or 'Go, sister' came from one woman sitting on the kerbstone with a baby on her knee whilst a group of some five or six men standing next to her were into whooping in a big way. One of them held out his hand as I ran past; I did the same and our hands came together at one hell of a speed. The man was larger than me by about 2 feet, certainly heavier by some 10 stone, and would have made Sonny Liston look like Madge Sharples. As I had just run 21 miles and, for all I know, he had just got out of bed, I would hazard a guess that I came off second best in this well-intentioned encounter. But the suspected broken arm and shattered hand at least gave me something to think about, as a change from the state of my weary legs.

During the last 5 or so miles of the London run my rhythm

and stride had gone completely, but I was still able to observe my surroundings. Here I was still running reasonably well, but the feeling of tiredness dominated any other sensation. I began to fail to see what was around me or to hear what was being said. I cannot remember the 2 or 3 miles through Harlem, between the point where I met the large black man with a hand clasp like a JCB and reaching the near side of Central Park. When I finally came to, it was because there were three fire trucks and two police cars with lights flashing and sirens wailing trying to overtake me on the outside, and even a legless, out-of-his-cups marathon runner could hardly fail to respond to that degree of intimidation.

I had at least reached Central Park. I tried to remember what I had said to Russell the other day, on the breakfast run . . . 'Just think, Russell, how good it will feel when we hit the park. Only 3 miles to go, and even that's through the nice parts.'

But it didn't feel good at all. There was no indication at that point that anything would ever feel good again. At the very time when I could have done with assistance and courtesy from the race organisers, they began messing about with hills. Fair enough, they did try to camouflage them by shipping in the rest of the world population apart from those previously passed, but no amount of subterfuge could convince my legs that they were not being asked to perform a bloody miracle.

If the crowds had not been there in such numbers to cheer and encourage me, I don't think I could have carried on. There were so many runners at the side of the road, so many walking, and try as I might, I couldn't find the words to help them on. The crowds tried very hard, however, telling them that it was 'very nearly over' and 'not to give up now', as if they felt that the runners were doing it on their behalf and that to see just one runner hit the dust was in some way a very deep, personal failure.

'It's on man, go it, you can do a sub 3.30, go, go, go, go!' And the hills seemed to go on and on between the crowds and the trees and above all this, when I could raise my head, were the tops of the tall buildings on Central Park South. So little way to

139

go, yet at no time was it possible to consider that I was going to finish.

I had reached a point where I felt that I had very little control over what my body was going to do during the next 2 miles. Not to finish now would be terrible — to have tried so hard and then just to pack in for a reason which I would never be able to understand. But it was impossible to think rationally or consider making a decision to do anything. So I kept moving.

I couldn't reply to the people who were willing me on. Yet I was so grateful that they were there. I couldn't even smile or wave or show the slightest sign of appreciation. All I could do was to keep moving and hope that that would be enough.

So much uncertainty at 25 miles. Again the shout of 'sub 3.30' and I tried to fathom out if that held any significance for me. But it must have done, because I felt my teeth come together a little tighter and I pushed and pushed up those interminable hills that felt like cliff faces but which could not have been more than mere gentle inclines.

I reached the end of East Drive and made the turn up Central Park South and began the last gruelling haul up to Columbus Circle, past the hotels on my left and the golden and green trees on my right. 'How do I keep running up here?' I had no idea. If I should suddenly stop now no one could surely blame me. I felt as if I had done all I was capable of doing. All I could do was to carry on doing whatever it was that I was doing, and wait and hope.

There was a quick diversion ahead as a runner hit the ground. As I reached him the poor bloke looked as if he wasn't breathing. His face was a dull grey when only a minute before it must have been the same throbbing red colour as my own. And he lay still, empty eyes facing the dull, empty sky as officials and police moved towards him.

'Oh God,' I thought, 'he's dead,' and all those selfish, greedy, unchristian thoughts flooded into my head which I seemed to remember from Sunday School, about how we should always help one another and not think of ourselves, and all I could think was, 'Oh, please God, don't let it happen to me, not here, not just before the end. Just let me finish, please let me finish.' But I could not conceive the outcome. It was no more certain now than it had been at the beginning of the race; and the people tried so hard to lift me, as if they had all done it before and knew how much it meant to have someone supporting, giving all that they could give.

Suddenly I saw Nick with his camera, where he had said he would be, at the base of Columbus Circle and I thought he had seen me. But the next time I lifted my head, some 30 yards from him, he was looking the other way. As I came to within a few yards I lifted both arms in the air for a short moment and watched thankfully as he dived for his camera and began shooting. I couldn't have looked at him or acknowledged him even if I had wanted to. I took the turn to the right, along the blue line that led back into Central Park.

I knew now how close the finish was. Once inside the park I would be able to see the stands that lined the last ½ mile, but still, incredibly, it was as if whoever was making this epic had forgotten to tell those taking part the rules governing when to run and when to stop. It surely was totally out of my control.

I don't remember crossing the small strip of grass seen many times during the previous week which led into the finishing stretch. The banner overhead read '26 miles' and then underneath 'just 385 yards' (or was it 'miles'? and a timing clock showed 3 hours, 28 minutes and 30 seconds. If I wanted to get round in less than 3½ hours all I had to do was keep moving for less than 1 minute and 30 seconds. I had no idea if that was possible.

The sound of the crowd was deafening. I thought of Pat in the stand somewhere, of the kids, of the camera crew and if they had made it and, if so, whether they would ever see me in the sea of runners which kept pouring into Central Park.

I had long since given up claiming any responsibility for what was going on. I thought of the film and pulled out my stupid, stupid white scarf and began waving, moved as far as I could to the left and ran and ran. I couldn't raise my head to look up or to the sides to see if anyone was there or not so I just aimed for the runner in front.

I looked up and saw the finish, the long thin blue banner stretching across the road. 'New York Road Runners' Club' it declared in large white lettering and listed the names of the sponsors. A second time clock showed 3.29.50 seconds and I closed my eyes and ran.

The next time I opened them the clock showed 3.29.53 seconds and I saw the wide blue line on the road in front which marked the finish.

And at 3.29.55 I crossed it.

Epilogue

Marshals, clad in bright yellow cagoules. Welcoming arms, for support or to hand out medals, decorated with red, white and blue ribbon.

'Ya look great...fantastic...congratulations,' said a lady as she hung one of the medals carefully over my head.

The computer strip was neatly torn off from the side of my running number. 'Well run, man,' said the voice as the strip was stacked in a long metal tube to be eventually sorted.

'Do ya wan' a medic?' Strong arms came around my shoulders. And me, leaning on the poor bloke in front, crying my eyes out and not being able to work out why.

Thousands of us, wandering in Central Park, holding bottles of Perrier water — a last present from one of the sponsors. Snugly wrapped in space blankets. Exhilarated. Proud expressions on tired faces.

I had finished in 4994th position. It was over, until the next time...